HEROINES
AN ATHOLOGY OF SHORT FICTION AND POETRY

Sarah Nicholson & Caitlin White
Editors

THE NEO PERENNIAL PRESS

Published by The Neo Perennial Press
Wollongong, Australia
www.theneoperennialpress.com

Copyright © 2018

All rights reserved.

National Library of Australia Cataloguing-in-Publication entry
Creator: Sarah Nicholson & Caitlin Wood
Title: Heroines: An anthology of short fiction and poetry / Edited by Sarah Nicholson and Caitlin Wood.
ISBN: 9780994645326
Subjects: Women--Fiction. Mythology. Fairytale. Folklore.

CONTENTS

- 3   *A Goddess Texts All her Exes*
- 4   *The Girl and the Narratorial Intrusion*
- 11 *Standing By*
- 12 *Light Dawns*
- 25 *Muse*
- 27 *Fairytale Endings*
- 34 *I Saw the Delphic Oracle*
- 35 *The Extra Chamber of My Heart*
- 40 *Requiem for Val*
- 41 *The Fisherman and the Cormorant*
- 46 *Midnight, Siren & Fire*
- 50 *The Menkas*
- 57 *Lilith*
- 58 *Bits and Bolds and Blood*
- 69 *Gorgon Girls*
- 71 *Juliet*
- 72 *Serendipity*
- 79 *Sapphic Hymn to Kali*
- 80 *Loving the Gorgon*
- 82 *Guinevere*
- 83 *Embroidered Map*
- 84 *Three Pieces of Gold, Three Pieces of Silver*
- 93 *Magnolia*
- 96 *Salt*
- 99 *Prologue*

The Goddess Texts All Her Exes
Maddie Godfrey

the goddess of loneliness sips her tea from the top of mountains. she leans back on a blanket fort of storm clouds, stares at her fingernails with the forgetfulness of humans. she conjures wine from the wells of mortal makers, stirs this liquid through the red sea until it tastes almost holy. soon she is slurring her wisdom into poetry. sketches Aphrodite from memory, spells her name wrong in the caption.

the goddess of loneliness opens Spotify and plugs her Aux cord into every streetlight. they flicker to the bass line of Nemesis' new diss track. the powerlines sag like frowns. she orders a burger on Chariot-Eats, curses the slow delivery time. tries to call Athena for a gossip session, but her owls answer instead. their hoots sound too much like pity.

the goddess of loneliness swipes through Tinder at 3:30am. Zeus sends her a pic of his lightning rod. Poseidon shares a string of wet emojis. Ares texts, "y u up so late?" and claims he has a motorcycle nearby. nobody asks her how soft the sky feels tonight. she dips her hands into the ocean, slips continents through the unoccupied spaces between her fingers.

the goddess of loneliness promises herself that she is still ethereal when reaching out. that being a little off balance does not mean you don't deserve a pedestal. she looks down at her armour and sees only vulnerability. does not know how honesty can form a force field. how petals are strong, not because of their substance, but because they regenerate.

the goddess is too human tonight. she does not want to sleep alone. she commands the sunrise to hurry. Helios says his chariot is busy fetching her a burger. she sighs, and for a moment, all mortals ache with her loneliness.

The Girl and the Narratorial Intrusion
Annika Herb

There was once a young girl, born to a fine, upstanding family of wealth and success. She had a delightful childhood, with everything she could ever want for provided to her. Her family loved her dearly; her parents doted on her. She grew into a kind, beautiful young woman, one who would one day make a fine wife and mother. But as she grew older, she began to long for something more, something outside the ivory walls of her home. She wanted adventure, to fight dragons and see the real world, to eat fruit she had grown herself.

Her parents were worried and they discussed it at length in their bedchambers. Her father was against the idea but his wife convinced him. She recognised the longing in her daughter's eyes, and she remembered what it had been like to be a young girl, so excited to see the world. And so, not wanting to trap their daughter, and as always, wanting desperately for her to have everything her heart desired, they kissed her brow and sent her out into the world.

The girl set off at dawn, brimming with excitement. The narrator decided to come along too and offer some useful advice, because sometimes they got really bloody sick of just watching these same old stories, you know?

It wasn't long until they came across a wizened old woman, begging at the steps of the church in the town centre.

"Ah, the locals are about," said the narrator. "Quick question before you run over there and demonstrate your ridiculously kind and trusting nature: have you been betrothed to any princes, lately?"

"No," said the girl.

"Carry on, then."

At once the girl fell to her knees in front of the old woman, clasping her hands.

"You poor thing! What fate has befallen you to leave you so?"

"My dear child, it is nothing but life; I am grateful to be able to sit in the sun, and be blessed by the kindness of passersby. I am fortunate; there is no need to cry for me so."

The girl drew out a loaf of bread, still warm and fresh from that morning. She pressed it into the woman's hands along with a gold coin, enough to buy a hundred more loaves.

"How are you with today's exchange rate?" the narrator enquired, but the girl didn't appear to hear them.

"Oh, thank you, sweet child," the woman cried. She waved to the girl and the narrator as they set off again.

"Why did you ask if I was betrothed, before?" the girl asked.

"Oh, it's no big deal. If you had been, the wizened old woman would have been a jealous stepmother or even a witch, come to poison or maim you to prevent you marrying her son and taking over the throne. As you're not, she's just your garden-variety beautiful wise witch disguised as a beggar woman. You showed her kindness, so I'm sure we'll run into her again when you're in a jam and she'll reward you, yada yada yada."

The girl had gone quite pale. "A stepmother—a w-witch?"

"Yes, well, it was pretty obvious, wasn't it? I even described her as wizened. If you're wizened, you're either a good or bad witch in disguise— or you're a rotting apple."

They continued on their way, the girl considering the narrator's clever words.

"What if I'd overlooked her completely, or been cruel?"

"Well, then you would've been looking at your stock standard vengeance/teaching curse. I mean, most of them say it's to teach you young upstarts a lesson, but we all know that it's more about the vengeance than anything else, don't we?"

As they walked further into town, they began to garner more stares. Well, the girl did, anyway, what with her rich clothes and long skirts and hair that had little to no lice in it.

A young boy, no more than five, ran up to the girl. He stared at her shyly, one thumb in his mouth and the other hand behind his back.

"Why hello," the girl said with a smile, crouching down to meet him. "How do you—oh!"

For the boy had thrown a handful of mud at her and snatched her ruby necklace from around her throat, then sprinted off.

The girl blinked up at the narrator.

"To be fair, you *were* wearing rubies," they reminded her. "Do you normally adorn yourself with fine jewels for hiking trips?"

"It was from my mother," the girl said sadly, and the narrator patted her hand.

"Never mind, I'm sure you'll come across it again at some point through some series of contrived coincidences. Speaking of, I suggest you start running."

The little boy had clearly fetched his older brothers to alert them of the rich lady in town; they entered the town square with eager eyes. The two ran, darting around corners and narrow laneways. As they passed an almost hidden doorway, a hand shot out and grabbed the girl's arm, dragging her inside. The narrator followed her in cheerfully.

"I'm sorry for startling you, young lady," their rescuer said. "I heard those boys chasing you, and I wanted to help."

"Oh, thank you ever so much!" the girl cried, wringing his hand. "You are a good man, sir."

"I am just a lowly shoemaker," the shoemaker said modestly. "Perhaps you have seen my work—your own father often commissions my services for your family."

"Of course!" the girl said warmly. "Why, you must be the finest shoemaker in all the land, and a hero to boot!"

"I love puns. I must try include them more often," the narrator said thoughtfully. "I do find it hard to slip them in, though." The other two ignored this.

"If you don't mind me asking, my lady, what are you doing outside of your castle walls?"

"I wanted to seek my fortune," the girl confided. Her eyes lit up. "I wanted to see the real world, to seek adventure." She wilted for a moment. "I suppose you must think this is all rather silly."

"Not at all!" the shoemaker cried warmly. The narrator sneezed. "In fact, my lady, let me help you on your way!"

"Oh, thank you, good shoemaker. I must say, I knew I was slightly naïve, but I wasn't expecting all that out there."

"Not to worry," said the shoemaker, rummaging through a closet. "We shall soon have you sorted. Here—some of my finest walking boots. Even if your body grows tired, your shoes will never weaken."

The girl thanked him and slipped her feet into the boots.

"Also," the shoemaker said. "Ah, well, you had better disguise yourself in these clothes of my son, and hide those locks under this cap. My wife will help you bind your chest, and we will smear ashes from the fireplace across your face to better hide your true nature."

Our lovely heroine blinked in confusion. "But why must I pretend to be a boy? Can I not dress as a peasant girl?"

The shoemaker shifted, looking uncomfortable. "Ah, well, my dear... we don't want to cause any unwanted attention, you see. A young girl, wandering the countryside by herself? You could be set on by thieves or vagabonds!"

"HE MEANS YOU'LL TOTALLY GET RAPED," the narrator explained helpfully.

"No, no, it's not that," the shoemaker hastened to say, glaring at the narrator when he thought the girl wasn't looking. "It's a safety precaution, yes, but it's also a grand tradition! Princesses and girls of noble stature have been coming through these parts for years, and they always dress up as boys to have adventures."

The girl frowned. "Why? Can't I head out and have an adventure on my own, without cross-dressing? Are you saying girls can't have adventures?"

"No," said the shoemaker.

"Yes," said the narrator.

"So what about when your wife goes out for a walk in the afternoons? Do you make her dress up in your clothes, as a 'safety precaution'?"

"No, not at all, my lady. For one thing, my wife would never take such a risk—walking around on her own through public spaces, indeed! You're a fanciful little thing, aren't you? What I mean to say is, only the silliest of girls would do such a thing on their own. They would have no one to blame but themselves if they were to be set upon!"

"I can't help but feel that your logic is flawed,"

said the narrator.

"And anyway," the shoemaker added reassuringly, "My wife is far too ugly and old to be attacked. Men only attack pretty young girls."

"Again, I don't think your logic checks out," the narrator said.

The girl frowned prettily. "And what do you mean, princesses and girls of noble stature? Don't girls from other classes go on adventures through here?"

"Well, not really, my lady. Exciting whims such as yours simply do not occur to those from simpler backgrounds. Simple backgrounds, simple minds, you know."

"They're generally too busy milking cows and supporting their families," explained the narrator.

The shoemaker barely suppressed a growl. "Do you mind?" he snapped at the narrator. "I am trying to uphold a grand tradition and help this lovely maiden on her way, and you are being really bloody annoying."

"Oh, shut up," the narrator said cheerfully, "or I'll write one of your appendages into a toad." Looking greatly offended, the shoemaker pressed his lips together tightly.

"Well," the girl said. "I suppose we best be on our way. Thank you for your hospitality."

The shoemaker glanced at the narrator before speaking. "Of course, my lady. Best wishes to you, from a humble shoemaker." He brightened. "I must warn you, before you go. On the edge of town, there are two roads that lead out into the country. One is longer, but it is safe. The other is far shorter, but on an abandoned path through a forest that is said to be haunted. Do not take that road—only death awaits you there."

The narrator looked at the girl. "Guess which road we're going to take. Go on. Take a guess."

"And watch out for devious creatures," the shoemaker said, ignoring the narrator. "They may try trick you and lure you into their traps. It's ogre season, too, and they'd just love a chance to gobble up a pretty little thing like you."

"Thank you for your advice," the girl said, "But I'm quite sure I can manage."

The narrator wisely refrained from pointing out that until two hours ago, she'd never even seen a rat. She'd thought it was some kind of malnourished rabbit and had tried to feed and sing to it. Luckily, there was no such thing as rabies in this story.

The shoemaker led them to the door. "Are you quite sure you don't want to wear the boys' clothes?" he asked sadly.

"Very sure," the girl said.

"But what about the vagabonds and thieves?" the shoemaker wheedled. He looked very disappointed at her refusal.

The narrator clapped. "Alright, that's it. You've got a toad. Toads for you."

The shoemaker turned an especially striking shade of puce and slammed the door. They could hear him cursing as they walked down the road.

"I didn't see any toad," the girl said, puzzled.

"Oh, don't worry, it was there," the narrator said brightly. "Just not anywhere you could see."

They set off towards the edge of town. As they walked, the buildings began to fall away, leading to more and more fields where sheep, horses, and the occasional unicorn grazed.

"These shoes are actually quite comfortable," the girl commented.

At last they came to a fork in the road. The road that veered off to the left was paved with golden bricks, and looked wide and clear. The road to the right had broken cobblestones twisting along its path, and quickly disappeared out of sight into a dark forest that loomed over their heads ominously. Whispers came from the blackened, gnarled trees.

"Hm," said the girl.

"It's a bit much, isn't it?" the narrator mused, a critical eye surveying the forest. "The glowing, sunlit path, and the creepy forest one with the sign that says DO NOT ENTER at the entrance. Might have gone a bit overboard there."

A lone crow screeched.

"I do think the crow's a nice touch. I deliberated between crow and raven—which one is creepier, do you think?"

"I want to go through there," the girl said.

The narrator grinned. "'Course you do. You don't want to try the easy-but-longer path first before something outside of your control steers you onto the shortcut?"

"Nope," the girl said. "Wait—give us a minute."

She strode over to the warning sign and snapped off the post, leaving the sign still propped up so all could see it. She hefted the stick into her hands: now she had a sharpened spear, ready to go.

"Resourceful," the narrator said. "I like that. Much more preferable than the idiotic ones who blindly decide to wander into the death-forest because it's shorter, and they think the little woodland animals will protect them, or the boring ones who decide to go on the nice, shiny path."

"I read a lot of books while I was safe in my family castle," the girl explained. "The characters never did what I wanted them to do. If I do this, I want to do things the way I want, because I choose them. And if I'm supposed to end up on this path anyway, I may as well do it of my own volition."

"Fair enough," the narrator said, nodding. "I should probably warn you then, that the chances of you encountering a malevolent forest spirit are high. You'll be confronted with thinly veiled metaphors so that you can grow as a person and ultimately become a well-rounded heroine, although really, it's a cookie-cutter set of attributes. And you're already so sweet and thoughtful that you don't have far to go."

The girl considered this for a moment. "Will I get to fight a dragon?"

"Most likely, yes, although you may defeat it with, you know, the power of words."

"Or a sword."

"Yes, or with a sword."

"Okay then," the girl said, smiling at the narrator. "Let's go."

And so, with the heroine swinging her spear and the clever narrator whistling merrily, they set off into the forest, ready to start a new story.

Standing By
Joyce Parkes

(*In memory of Margaret Button who would lean
on argument – quote or question friend and foe*)

Margaret, friend, foe, critic, furthered argument
with one of Aristotle's writs: *Without courage
there is no virtue*. An insight, she continued,
which may have prodded Scott to write: *Show me
a hero and I will write you a tragedy*, which may

have nudged Zelda to recall Socrates' finding:
the unexamined life is not worth living — urging
Margaret and Jo to mull over William's given:
*All the world's a stage and all the men and women
merely players*, where Noel Coward sang: *Don't

put your daughter on the stage, Mrs Worthington*.
And although Yeats saw *the folly of being comforted*,
Rilke felt *that in the end, all we have are our
vulnerabilities*. Leaving White to write: *So that
in the end there was no end.** Standing by the window

of culture and the arts led Jo to question why
a woman's insights, outlook, adventures, pleas
for understanding, opinions, tropes, are a tenth,
at most, of published texts quoted (in and out
of context) in countries claiming gender parity.

* From *The Tree of Man* by Patrick White

Light Dawns
Julie Kearney

And Lo! The Hunter of the East has caught
The Sultan's Turret in a Noose of Light.
  —The Rubaiyat of Omar Ahayyám

Edward Liddell, born in England but still eligible in the first decades after India's independence to be made a bishop of the Church of South India, was not a worldly man, especially when it concerned his daughter. In fact, in everything concerning Nalini he was a doting fool. Sitting at his big teak desk he frowned and tapped his Waterman pen on the blotter. Arranging a marriage wasn't a man's job and more than ever Bishop Liddell missed Vijaya who had known it to be hers.

Vijaya never had any doubts about how to find a husband for their daughter. Before her shockingly sudden death from a heart attack she had sat at the computer every morning, scrolling through prospective grooms on the Anglo-Indian matrimonial websites. None had met with Nalini's approval. Too fat, too old, too ugly—no one pleased their precious girl.

Born to them in later life, the Liddell's only child was beautiful, willful and clever. Having completed her BA she intended further studies and it was accepted that whoever she married must fall in with these plans. But married she must be. At twenty-two, time wasn't on her side. Bishop Liddell sighed and took up his pen.

Dear Cousin Nita . . . He penned a paragraph of greetings and chewed his lip as he came to the nub of the matter:

Nalini tells me that Griffith University in your city offers an excellent course in cross-cultural feminist theory, which she hopes to enroll in. But her mother also had a dearly held wish which was to see our little Nellie married. This is a difficult subject to broach, but I was wondering if you might have some suggestions regarding a suitable . . .

Nita replied with the promptness of a woman called upon to match-make. Bishop Liddell scanned the letter.

. . . arranged marriages aren't the way here of course but as it happens I do have someone who might meet with

your approval—John's nephew, Harry King. Dr King, actually. (I've enclosed a photo of him taken at our last Christmas party.) Harry lectures at the same university Nalini wishes to attend. To be honest, I must tell you we're a little worried about him lately. He's become quite reclusive since that wretched wife of his left him. Is that a problem for you by the way? They're divorced now and there are no children to complicate matters. Finding the right woman would be just the thing for Harry, and Nalini is such a lovely girl. John and I were quite taken with her when we visited last year...

    Bishop Liddell felt his skin crawl. Perhaps it wasn't such a good idea after all. And Nalini had just told him she liked the fellow's photo.

    'But it's only a photo and you'll be going so far. Let's find out more about this chap first.'

    'No, Daddy-ji. I told you, I like him. Ask Cousin Nita to do her stuff.' Nalini arched her toes on the floor, looking thoughtfully at their painted nails. Outside the windows the coconut palm fronds shivered as if in sympathy.

Dear Edward,
Well I'm afraid you won't like my news. I went over to Harry's place—he's holed up there now he's on sabbatical, writing some book or other—and the upshot is he's agreed, but with one proviso. He's prepared to marry Nalini but in name only. He said he quite understood a bright young student in a developing country might want to further her studies and if the antiquated notions of her father—you must remember Harry is Australian so please don't take offence—if that meant she wasn't allowed unless as a married woman, it was no skin off his nose etc. etc. I believe he thought he was striking a blow for something. So, of course, I said that wasn't ...

    Bishop Liddell threw down the letter. Insolent pup! How dare he insult Nalini with such a proposal. A marriage in name only indeed!

    But when he told Nellie at dinner that night she laughed.

    'Don't worry, Daddy.'

    Bishop Liddell spluttered. 'Don't worry? I'm surprised you aren't insulted.'

    'On the contrary, I think it's all gone very well. Just as I like in fact.'

'Good heavens, how has it gone well and not badly? The proposal that man has made is dishonorable.'

Nalini jumped up from her chair. Her red sari shimmered like a flame. She stamped her slender foot on the polished tiles, her dark eyes flashed, her lips pouted.

'Honour schmonner! Honestly, Daddy, if you understood men you'd know he's not called King for nothing.' She pulled Harry King's photo from her tight *choli* and waved it at her father. 'Can't you see? He's a king among men.'

Bishop Liddell stared at the limp, breast-warmed photo, then at Nalini who was laughing.

'Don't think twice about it,' she told him. 'I'm going to Brisbane and when I get there we'll see how long Dr King wants a marriage in name only.'

At dawn the first rays of the sun struck rainbow-colored light from the beveled edge of the wardrobe mirror. Harry opened one eye to scowl at it. He groaned, groped for his jogging pants lying beside the bed, shrugged them on and stumbled out to the kitchen.

Through the French doors came assorted warblings and twitterings. A vista of smoke-blue hills framed in leafy light pressed up at the window but Harry didn't glance at it. He'd seen the view often enough in the five years he and Evelyn had lived in this converted farmhouse on the outskirts of Brisbane. Not that he noticed anything much these days; he was too busy working on his manuscript. Today was the first of September, most of his sabbatical gone and the bloody thing was still dragging. He carried his coffee out to the veranda and sat staring blankly at the trees. Slivers of light pushed above the eastern hills and the whole valley trembled in welcome with the tiny movements of millions of back-lit leaves. The only thing not moving was Harry.

A car was coming up the driveway. A red Astra. Who on earth? At this hour?

He watched the car crawl towards the house. It stopped and a young woman wearing a sari got out. *Christ!* Not that Indian student. He'd made it clear to Aunt Nita he wasn't to be bothered by her. It was strictly a Clayton's marriage so the girl could study in

Australia. He was already having misgivings about his grand gesture and now for God's sake, it looked like she was coming out here to bother him. Well, he'd soon get rid of her.

He stood up and walked to the edge of the steps.

The girl wore a deep blue sari with a shiny gold hem. A tinkling sound came from the bangles on her arms as she walked towards him. She looked up and smiled. 'I was hoping it wasn't too early but I see you're up already.'

She came up the steps and put out her hand. 'Hello. I'm Usha, pronounced as in bush.' Her red lips curved in a smile. 'Usha Saraswati.'

'Saraswati?' Harry was relieved. 'You, er, you're not related to Professor Saraswati by any chance, are you?'

Usha nodded. 'His daughter actually. I have him to thank for my divine name.'

'It is? Er, won't you sit down?' He gestured at the table. Best not invite her in the house.

'Yes, all Daddy's fault,' she said, sinking into a chair. 'Usha is the Dawn Goddess and Papa saw fit to name me after her.' She laughed. 'And here I am, visiting you at dawn.'

Harry nodded, a little dazed by her smiles.

'I'm a friend of Nalini Liddell's,' she went on. 'My father and hers are old friends so of course we offered to put her up.'

'Right.' Harry realized he was staring at her. She was extraordinarily pretty, but then Indian girls often were. 'Sorry. Would you like a drink? Tea, coffee?'

'I'd love a coffee. I've just come off night shift and I'm exhausted.'

She looked cool and self-possessed and not exhausted at all.

'I'm a nurse at the Retirement Village down the road so it was easier to drop by on my way home. Coffee would be great.'

When he came back from the kitchen Usha was staring at a magpie on the railing. He passed her the mug and sat down. 'So you've come about your friend?'

'Yes. Nalini wanted me to bring you this.' Usha opened her shoulder-bag and brought out a spray of jasmine which she put on the table. The starry white flowers with their delicate pink throats lay there looking absurdly feminine and frivolous. An almost indecently languorous scent floated to Harry's nostrils. He drew back, offended.

'A flower?'

'It's traditional where she comes from. The bride must send gifts to her betrothed for five days before the wedding.'

'There's no need for that.' Harry frowned. 'After all, the marriage is just a formality.'

Usha nodded. 'Nalini wants to do it for her mother's sake. Vijaya, that's her mother, would have been upset if she omitted the custom. We talked it over and Nalini decided, since it's not a proper marriage, she needn't send anything of value. She hopes you will accept these forest flowers instead.'

'Well I'd rather she didn't just the same. Isn't her mother dead anyway? So, um, Miss Liddell doesn't have to worry.'

'That's not the point. Just because her mother is ...'

Usha looked down at her lap, playing with her fingers. When she looked up her face was stiff, almost masklike. 'It might be polite to show some sensitivity regarding her feelings, don't you think?'

Harry assumed a solemn face, realizing he'd been politically incorrect. 'Of course, if it's the custom where Nalini comes from.'

'So, shall we say each morning around this time? It would suit me and if you're not up I'll just leave the flowers here. On this table.'

Usha stood up and stretched out her hand. The gold border of her sari, falling across her arm, caught fire in the slanting dawn light, momentarily dazzling him.

'It's up to you what you do with them after that. You can throw them away if you wish, but at least Nalini will know she's doing her duty.'

Harry watched Usha's bum as she went down the path, watched her wriggle her bum into the Astra, watched the Astra disappear down the driveway. He picked up the jasmine, tossed it over the railing and went inside. A pushy young thing, he decided as he poured out muesli. After breakfast he rang his aunt to complain about the intrusion on his privacy.

'Does Professor Saraswati have a daughter?' Nita said vaguely. 'I thought it was just the two boys. Well, that's nice. It'll be good for Nalini to have a girlfriend to help her adjust. Not that she needs much help there, I must say. Did you know she's already getting herself about in a car? She drove over for dinner the other day in a ...'

'But Nita,' interrupted Harry, 'it's a bit much if I'm to be constantly visited by her friend. I didn't expect this when I offered to help out and I can tell you I don't appreciate it.'

'Well it won't be for long, only four more days. You can cope with that surely? Now don't forget, it's ten o'clock at the Customs House. I think I told you that.'

'Of course, I won't forget.' Harry hated the way Aunt Nita talked to him as if he was still a child.

'And perhaps if you wore a suit. I know it's none of my business but it would look better wouldn't it? We don't want Nalini thinking Australians are uncouth.'

'Mmm . . . sure . . . well I'd better keep going, Nita. Busy day.' Harry hung up in no better mood than when he began.

Next morning, gloomily spooning up muesli, he heard a car. That woman again? He wiped his mouth and went out to investigate. Yes, the Astra. He looked at his watch. Six forty. The sun was just rising, throwing a band of pale light across the valley. Two rosella parrots swooped over the Astra and landed in the grevillea bush beside the steps, making soft clucking sounds as they inched towards the flowers. Somewhere in the distance magpies caroled.

Usha came quickly up the path. Her sari, a gauzy peach color today, was half hidden by yellow wattle.

'I had to pick so many,' she said, glancing down when she saw Harry looking. 'The trees are so bursting it seemed mean not to be generous.'

She put the flowers on the table where they lay in a circle of pollen dust. He noticed a smudge of it on her cheek, which for some reason was charming, though not charming enough. He knew he would have to offer her coffee and get involved in meaningless chit-chat.

'Cup of coffee?' he said, making off through the French doors without waiting for a reply.

She followed him to the doorway.

'Please don't bother. I know you're busy.' She looked around the room.

'Come in. It's no trouble. I was going to have another one anyway.'

He might just as well, he thought, filling the electric jug. He had no intention of going to the bother of getting out the percolator. He watched Usha drift round the room, her sari shimmering whenever she paused in one of the bars of light streaming through the windows. She picked up a book from the coffee table and made a space for herself among the ones on the couch. Reading now. At least she wasn't in a talkative mood today. She was still reading when he brought over the mugs.

'Thanks.' She held up the book. 'This looks interesting. Is it part of what you're studying?'

Harry sat down across from her. 'It throws a little light on what I'm writing about.'

'Which is?'

'Post-modernist theory you could call it, in so far as that term has any meaning.' He paused. What was he doing, gabbing about post-modernism to a nurse who'd just come off night duty?

Politely he stifled a yawn. As often happened these days, ever since Evelyn decamped, he had slept badly. He noticed the cushions Usha was leaning against, the ikat cushions Evelyn had bought on their honeymoon in Bali. He remembered how she had spread them out on bed to admire and he'd pushed her down on them and made love to her. Harry's eyes, travelling upwards, encountered Usha's, and he realized he'd been staring at her hips outlined against the cushions.

She looked at him thoughtfully, then at the book. 'Intellectual Impostures,' she said, reading out the title. 'Ideas pretending to be what they're not I suppose. Is that it, Dr. King?'

'More or less.' He shifted in his seat. 'It's written by two mathematicians, objecting to the way some academics borrow terms from science and apply them to their own areas of study.'

'You mean like Kristeva's use of maths to describe poetry? What do they say about that?'

Harry did a double-take. 'You're into Kristeva?'

'Only because Nalini is always talking about her,' Usha wrinkled her nose. 'Kristeva's difficult, don't you find?'

In no time at all Harry found himself launched on a sea of Derrida-speak while his coffee grew cold and scummy on the table. Usha had an excellent understanding of the functional limits of metaphor and he had just reached an interesting point he wanted to make when she stood up and announced she must go.

She gestured at the windows, now filled with sunlight. 'My namesake has departed,' she said, smiling, 'so this Usha must depart too.'

Brushing aside his protests, she prepared to leave. He watched the little ritual of sari-patting and hair-smoothing, and when it was over he walked her out to her car.

Spring in Brisbane is not a particularly noticeable event. The weather grows warmer, certain flowers appear, but it is not the spring you read about in the northern hemisphere—the beginning of new life after a hard, cold winter. Brisbane winters are never hard or cold. When he woke up next morning Harry decided dispensing with the blanket was overdue. He went into the kitchen where he smelled the mock orange outside the window and decided to clean his teeth. While he was cleaning his teeth he decided to find a clean shirt, but the reason for these decisions did not impinge on his consciousness.

Sitting on the veranda in a clean shirt with clean teeth, he looked out at the wooded hills. A bird was calling, distinct from all the rest, four notes rising except for the last which fell away in a dying cadence, like the embodiment of longing. Over and over the Liddell-like tones sounded, remote and distilled by distance. Harry had the sensation of being caught and held in the moment, pinned by the notes of the invisible bird. For the first time in a long while he noticed the light on the leaves. Overhead, small fluffy clouds tinged with gold floated in a sky of baby-blue. Canaletto clouds, he thought idly. Downstairs in the computer room work was waiting but Harry gave no thought to it as he usually did at this hour. The clinking of frogs came up from the creek and he wondered if they really were frogs or if they were toads. In his present mood he preferred to think they were frogs. It went with the morning which was hopeful, calmly expectant, waiting for the sun to rise.

The clouds were now palely, ecstatically gold and he stared at them in surprise, even a little wonder. Time to make a move, he decided. The Astra appeared at the gateway and began crawling up the driveway like an industrious red beetle.

That night Harry dreamed he was running. In his dream he came to the base of a hill that rose in a perfect hemisphere, a child's drawing of a hill, a hill like a breast. He began to run up its grassy flank and found he was flying, or not quite flying but floating up the hill and the sensation of joy this gave was very sweet. He saw that Usha was floating beside him, the two of them moving together towards the crest of the hill. They were almost there when he began to lose speed; he was not going to make it and his disappointment was intense. Usha looked back and held out her hand. He grasped it and together they floated to the top of the hill.

Harry woke with a feeling of euphoria and immediately realized he was in love with Usha Saraswati. And just as quickly remembered that in two day's time he was to marry Nalini Liddell.

Bloody hell.

But even this thought couldn't dispel the delicious feeling the dream had left behind. He would not think, he could not think, until he'd made himself a coffee.

Ten minutes later, sitting on the veranda, he still couldn't think. There was nothing to think, and even if there were, he couldn't think anyway because the whole crazy fact of Usha pushed all other thoughts aside. He lusted for her, that much was certain. He was also about to marry another woman and there wasn't a dead dog's chance of getting out of it. Harry knew himself trapped. He had made a promise and must keep it.

He listened for Usha's car. A number of cars went by but none were hers. At eight o'clock he cursed the world and all its misbegotten inhabitants and went downstairs to the computer-room where he spent a miserable, unproductive morning.

At midday he was upstairs again, slumped on the couch in the living room, apathetically picking at a cheese sandwich when Mrs Ford came bustling into the room.

'Shift your feet, Dr. King,' she ordered. 'I gotta get this room done before I start downstairs.'

A small dumpy woman with a high, unhealthy color, she began sweeping under Harry's raised feet and engaging him in conversation. 'How's the book coming along? Nearly finished I s'pose.'

Mrs Ford liked Dr. King and had noticed his glooms ever since that wife of his upped and left him. That Call-me-Mrs-King woman who no longer was. Each cleaning day Mrs Ford saw the pile-up of empty bottles on the kitchen bench and wished something would come into Dr. King's life to cheer him.

'Still working on it, Mrs Ford,' muttered Harry.

'Complicated plot is it?'

'Not really.' *Yes, really.* He knew the evasion was patronizing but the thought of discussing post-modernism with Mrs Ford was too awful to contemplate.

'What's this then?'

Mrs Ford's broom had hooked an earring from under the couch. She picked it up and eyed it severely as if demanding an explanation from it. Perhaps Dr King had a friend, which would be all to the good in her opinion. The secrets of his bedroom were known to her and she knew no woman except herself had been there since Evelyn. She handed him the loop of gold.

'Someone will be missing that, you can bet your bottom dollar.'

She watched him attentively, noticing the way he stared at it, noting also that he pocketed it with a furtive air. She was instantly alerted.

'Whose could that be I wonder? That's an expensive piece of jewelry that is. The owner will be looking everywhere.'

Long experience told Harry she wouldn't give up. 'It belongs to a friend of mine.'

'Well that's good.' Mrs Ford began sweeping again. 'Nice to know you're having friends over.' She eyed him shrewdly.

'Not a friend exactly. Just ah . . . a messenger.'
'A courier?'
'No. Well, yes, sort of.'
'That would be papers from the university then?'

Harry wasn't going to explain the details of his private life to Mrs Ford. He knew if she had any inkling he was about to marry a woman he'd never met, she would be appalled. He felt the same way.

'We, uh, we just talk.'

'Talking's good.' Mrs Ford continued sweeping. 'It never hurts to talk. Get a few things aired, get them off your chest.'

'I suppose so,' said Harry, adding, 'She brings me flowers.'

Mrs Ford was confused. 'I didn't know you'd took up gardening,' she ventured.

Suddenly Harry found he was unburdening himself. 'I haven't, but the thing is, I don't know what to do about it.'

Mrs Ford was so astonished she stopped sweeping. 'You don't know what to do? I'd of thought you'd know most things.'

She spoke truthfully. She was deeply suspicious of this mystery woman who was coming to Dr. King's house and upsetting him.

'And do you give her anything in return?'

Harry felt a rush of gratitude. *Of course*. It was all one-sided.

The dawn chorus was getting under way, the sun nudging hills dreaming under veils of blue. Luminous ribbons of light fell across the grassy lower slopes. It was the morning before the day Harry was to marry Nalini Liddell. In the kitchen he put freshly-ground coffee in the percolator. A jug of red roses stood on the bench. The familiar sound of the Astra reached his ears and he grabbed the flowers and hurried out to the veranda.

'Come in, come in. You're just in time for coffee.' She was wearing apple green today, very fetching. He held out the roses but she made no move to take them.

'For you, Usha.'
'You mean for Nalini.'

'No, for you.' Harry smiled extravagantly. 'I'll put them in water, shall I? Where would you like to sit? Oh, is that a water-lily?' He saw she was putting down a flower.

'It's a lotus. From Nalini.' Her clipped tones told her annoyance.

They both looked at the lotus which lay on the table as though floating, its petals seeming to give off light.

'Uh, thanks. I mean, please thank Miss Liddell for me.'

He pulled out a chair for her. 'Have a seat. I'll get the coffee.'

When the coffee was on the table he drew up his chair. 'I was thinking, if you're not busy today, if you like, maybe—'

'If you're asking me out, Dr King, I'm afraid the answer is no. Aren't you forgetting you're getting married tomorrow?'

'But—'

'I don't go out with married men, not even ones who won't sleep with their wives.'

Harry protested. 'But surely Miss Liddell has told you it's just an arrangement. It means nothing to either of us.'

'I'm sorry but that's how it is.'

He slumped in his chair and as if in triumph at his defeat a magpie began caroling.

'So lovely,' breathed Usha, leaning forward to peer at the fig tree outside the veranda. 'Madge-pies have beautiful songs.'

Madge-pies?

Suspicion slithered into Harry's brain. He tried to calculate. To his knowledge Professor Saraswati had been teaching history at Griffith Uni for decades, which meant Usha was brought up in Australia. So what was this madge-pie business?

'And how do you think they compare with the bakerbirds?'

'The bakerbirds?' She hesitated.

'Yes.' He gestured at the fig tree where a family of butcherbirds were enjoying a game of chase. 'Their song is beautiful too.'

'Oh, the bakerbirds. Yes, they're lovely.'

'Liar!' Harry leapt to his feet. 'What the hell's going on? Who are you anyway?' His heart was jumping.

'Who am I?' She too had risen. Her pupils were dilated. 'Can't you guess?'

'What?' He took a step towards her, glowering. 'I don't—' He breathed heavily. 'Oh God!' He let out a shuddering sigh. '*You*. You're her! I mean she's you. I'm marrying you.'

She smiled faintly. 'Does that please you?'

'I'm marrying you,' he repeated slowly. Tentatively he put his arms around her, breathing her scent. He started kissing her, her ear, her cheek, her lips but she was pulling away.

'No Harry, wait. Just let me—wait I said! I have to make a call.'

She had her mobile out and was busy keying numbers.

'A phone call?' Harry was shell-shocked. 'Then you'd better, you'll have to go outside. The reception isn't too good here.'

Dazed, he followed her down the steps.

'Hello, Daddy. Did I get you up? No, everything's fine. Yes, tomorrow. No, it'll be just as you wish, a proper marriage. Yes, of course there'll be a party afterwards. Mrs Saraswati and Cousin Nita have seen to that. Would you like to speak to Harry? He's here beside me.'

She handed Harry the phone. Above them in the fig tree, the magpie burst into song.

Muse
Sarah Rise

I wonder whether Clio
if she's not too busy
with that unwieldy trio
of Word, Event, Grand Narrative
Beating drum to relentless march of Time
Wiping down the slaughter-bench of History
Sorting victors' voice from victims' voice
retelling, recalling, recounting
If she's not too tired
from spanning and scanning
the Centuries from end to end
juggling the players and powers
of each town and epoch
place and period
Wooed by Kings and Popes
and Peoples with a Capital
her legs spread across the seas and seasons
through spells of plenty and want
recording those great bright clashes of Mankind
the might and fight and spill of it all
When she has folded
the hundred-told stories
into Her-story
will Clio
if I bring her honey-melon
bathe her feet
and sing to her on moonlit nights
or better, offer myself to her
as scribe or record-keeper
will she repay me
with the small story of me
my mother and father
my house
my own brief path
the history of this day
this Tuesday perhaps
or this afternoon
this place
this table – too small, do you think,
for a history?
Oh muse
Oh mystery

Oh mistress
tell me the tale of me
my here and now.

Fairy tale Endings
Emily Brewin

Prince Charming does yoga. At least, this one does. He looks princely enough, with his head of dark hair and piercing blue eyes. He scans the room for a spot on the floor, mat rolled tight in his hand like a sceptre.

I try to catch his eye. I wouldn't say no, even though I don't believe in fairy tales. I hate the way the princesses in them always need a bloke to save them. I'm more a Patti Smith girl myself.

Anoushka sits cross-legged on one side of me, meditating with her eyes closed. Usually I prod her if she's taking too long but this time I let her sit. The longer she remains in a vegetative state the better.

Around us, the studio is packed, as always. But there's a wedge of floor on the other side of me that I'm sure Prince Charming could squeeze into.

'Can you move over?' I say to cat-pose lady on the mat next door. She gives me a look as I slide her drink bottle away.

The cloying scent of deodorant mixed with the odd puff of patchouli infuses the room. It's hot, and damp patches are already forming under my arms. I wish Instructor Teagan would turn the fan on. If I'd wanted to do Bikram I would have gone to the studio down the road where the real fanatics go.

Teagan pats Prince Charming on the shoulder, making him jump. 'Find a spot, please,' she says.

'Here', I call loudly 'Over here.'

Cat-pose lady rolls her eyes but I don't care, Prince Charming is walking my way. On arrival, he reveals a neat set of teeth but doesn't quite smile at me. Anoushka stirs. I ignore her and hope he does too.

After a stretch, Teagan tells us to partner-up.

'Hi'. Noush stands, with legs like stilts and breasts that defy gravity. She beams at Prince Charming. Unlike me, she loves the idea of being a princess. But I suppose that's what happens when your dad deserts you as a kid.

The Prince clears his throat.

Bitch, I think without malice. It's just the way she is.

Teagan calls Anoushka to the front of the room to help her demonstrate a twin warrior pose. And for once I'm glad for my friend's remarkable flexibility.

I give Noush a small wave then move in on the Prince before cat-pose lady nabs him. Suddenly, I'm happy I had the foresight to shave my underarms this morning.

The Prince and I come together and pull apart and brace against each other in what could be considered foreplay. He exhales in my face, breath minty as toothpaste. I consider the flimsiness of the fabric separating our skin and my palms grow sweaty.

'Sorry'.

He wipes his hands on his pants. 'It's natural.'

I detect an accent, French, I think, and blush. The way he says natural invokes visions of nudity.

Noush stays with Teagan until the end of class, wowing the rest of us with their perfectly composed flying bow and their double gate pose.

We wrap up with a backbend. I usually opt out, but Prince Charming is watching so I ease over, ignoring the pain in my spine.

'I'm Bec,' I grimace.

'Jacques,' he says, looking down at me from an angle that's unnerving.

I lower myself to the ground.

'You want to show me where people drink around here?'

It sounds more like a command than a question.

I giggle, a nervous habit, and glance down at my stretched gym top. 'Sure', I shrug. 'There's a place down the road that doesn't have a dress code.'

At the bar, I search my purse for change. Jacques has ordered the most expensive cocktail on the menu. Maybe he really is a prince. Now there's only enough money left for two pots of lager.

I deliver the cocktail, 'Ta da', and take a seat opposite him, hoping Noush takes her time in the loo. Jacques's wallet is lying open on the table between us. There's a crisp fifty-dollar note tucked behind a business card with the name Victor de Gavre on the front of it.

He sees me and closes the wallet.

I smile sweetly. He can get the next round.

'You like this beer'. He points at the glasses in front of me. 'Australian beer tastes a bit like piss.'

I cough.

He takes a lingering sip of his cocktail and scans the room.

'That's better.' Noush comes back, transformed out of her gym gear.

'Great'. I say flatly, wishing I'd brought a change of clothes too.

'Beer?' She sits opposite and raises a brow in a way that makes her almond shaped eyes even more alluring. The sight of her still manages to take my breath away sometimes. I don't bother looking at Jacques. I can guess how he's reacting.

At university, guys would stop mid-conversation with me to gape at Anoushka. I could have done backflips. It wouldn't have mattered. Everyone wanted her. Even the lesbian collective invited her to their fundraisers.

All through our twenties and early thirties, she left men scattered in her wake while my love life floundered. She's a goddess, like Artemis with a bit of Aphrodite thrown in. That's what the lesbians said, anyway. None of it does her any good though. She always ends up with losers.

I down my drink. 'It's all I could afford', I say, loudly.

Noush's perfume cuts through the fuggy bar air. Jacques has probably fallen off his chair by now. I wonder meanly if now is the time to bring up her eating problems. But then she gives my arm a rub, and I recall how sick she gets and how much I love her.

I brave a look at Jacques. To my surprise he seems unmoved. He just crosses his legs in a way that causes his gym shorts to ride up his muscular thighs. I'd like to put my hand up there; even though he's obviously a twit.

Anoushka seems blind to the fact. She pouts and asks if he'd like another cocktail instead.

'Qui,' he says, flicking a hand at his empty glass.

'A *Vieux Carré*', I say, when she looks perplexed. 'And, I'll have a vodka and orange'. I push my beer glass away.

Noush comes back with our drinks, her dress clinging to her hips and a smile like the dazzling sun. It does the trick. Jacques grins in return and I'm back to being the ugly stepsister again.

'Think I'll go home,' I say, sculling the vodka and tucking my gym top in.

I go to yoga every evening for two whole weeks after that night, determined to improve myself. It almost kills me but I can bend backwards without resuscitation and a new bloke joins the class. He's Canadian.

I don't see Jacques again, but I know what he's doing because he's plastered all over Noush's Facebook page. I stalk them. There they are at the botanic gardens, Anoushka an angel in white, Jacques beside her in loafers. And again, on a sundrenched deck; Noush cosying into Jacques, who has a vacant look on his face that makes me uncomfortable.

There are phone calls too, late at night. I drift off to Noush's exaltations about her new boyfriend's stylish wardrobe and refined tastes, which I'm sure is code for expensive.

'It's intense', she says in a way that makes my eyes flick open.

I recognise the tone in her voice but stop short of asking if she's still eating properly.

The next time I see them, Noush is attached to Jacques's arm. She's arranged lunch at the boathouse so her friends can meet him. Their combined beauty is like a blinding light. It makes everything else seem drab.

'Good to see you', I say to Jacques while Noush mingles.

He gives me a cursory glance then goes back to watching her laugh with a waiter.

'Looks like she's having fun.'

'Maybe', he replies, before walking away.

I flirt with a university pal and keep an eye on Anoushka. There's a new thinness to her arms and she keeps checking in with Jacques, who sits sulkily in a corner.

'I'm exercising more,' she says when I take her aside. 'Jacques likes me to stay fit.'

I frown but she makes an excuse and strides away.

Jacques's aloofness seems to attract women. They flock to him at the party, lashes aflutter, retreating soon after, smaller than before. Anoushka spends much of her time rubbing his arm. And, at the end of the day she picks up his bill.

She disappears for a couple of months after the boathouse and doesn't return my calls. There's nothing on Facebook. When I knock on her front door, the lights upstairs flick off and the place falls silent. I knock loudly until the lady next door tells me to pipe down. Then I walk away again, angry for trying.

Finally, she calls to cancel a long-standing dinner date.

'I'm spending too much,' she says, flatly.

'I'll pay'. I say, wondering how much he's costing her.

The line muffles but I hear the drone of voices.

'I can't', she says, finally. 'Jacques isn't well.'

'C'mon Noush'. 'I'm exasperated. 'Surely he can manage for one night on his own.'

'Sorry'. She hangs up without a goodbye.

Riled, I decide to research her Prince Charming. I start with Google. Jacques's surname is *Bonny*. It seems ironic.

There's more than one. Among them, an American asparagus farmer and heavy metal fan from Berlin. I narrow it to France and find a teacher in Lyon and a graphic design student in Marseille. They don't fit the bill. I search for over an hour, without much luck.

I tap my forehead. Jesus, what am I doing? It's time Noush grew up and stopped falling for morons. Because that's all Jacques is after all, I think; a daft, cheapskate...

Something clicks. I recall the night in the bar after yoga, the open wallet and crisp fifty-dollar bill. There was a business card he seemed intent on hiding. I stare at the wall above my computer, covered in free postcards from the cafes I visit. My favourite features a unicorn galloping through the night sky. A creature too good to be true. The name on the card. What was it? Vern or Van. Something unusual. I tap my forehead. Think. And, get out of my seat. Think. The radio in the kitchen down the hall hums low and indiscernible as I pace the room. The name hovers at the edge of my memory, shifting about so I can't pin it down.

Varn, Vin, Vinc.

I wish I hadn't thrown the Sudoku book Mum gave me for Christmas in the bin. My brain's clearly undernourished.

Val, Vaughn.

I stop pacing and inhale.

Victor… Victor de Hollier.

I sit down again and type the name, slowly, into Google. Half way down the first page, I see it. *Victor de Hollier. Soldat. Armée belge.* I channel Madame Leblanc, my year eight French teacher, and translate. *Soldat*, it either means real estate agent or soldier. Armée belge, is Belgian Army, I think. I click. A photo of Jacques appears.

He's wearing a brown beret and is holding a rifle. The shadows on his face make it hostile. The gun doesn't help. I think of Noush, soft as a shellfish, and my heart contracts.

Under the photo, there's an entry written in French. The word *gendarmerie* pops up too many times for my liking. Police. I click the next link. It's him again, and this time the entry is in English. It was posted nine months ago. The words blur as I read them.

When I call Anoushka, he answers.

'Qui?' he says.

There's silence as I try to steady my breath.

'Qui, Qui?' he repeats, clearly annoyed.

'Jacques', I say, lightly, 'Is Noush there?'

'It is late,' he sounds irritated.

I struggle to stop my hand shaking. Visions of Noush rush though my head. I should have knocked harder on her door that night or insisted she come for tea. I think of the last time she was in hospital, trying to convince her to eat, to live. A get-well card from her father sat on the table beside her bed. I read it. He was too busy to visit.

'I've done something to my back, Jacques', I say. Two can play his game. 'I need help.'

He takes a moment, and I have to stop myself from begging.

He puts the phone down. 'Anoushka!' he yells.

'Yes?' She answers, finally.

It's a far cry from her usual greeting but the sound of her voice makes my heart sing.

'It's me', I say, in my best sick-day voice. 'Can you come over?'

I can almost hear the cogs turning, the excuses

she plans to make.

'Hold on'.

She whispers something to Jacques, and I think I've lost her.

'Okay,' she says, slowly. 'Jacques will drive me.'

It takes all my might not to ask why she can't drive herself, but I just say, 'thanks', and hang up the phone.

I sit for a moment, staring at the words on the screen. *Ex-soldier bashed girlfriend to near death.*

I'm almost numb with fear and fury, but I force myself to move.

'Salaud', I say to the photo of the man with the beret cocked on his head like a crown. Bastard. Then I pick up the phone again and call the police.

I Saw the Delphic Oracle
Toni Brisland

sitting on a milk crate in an all-girls school yard,
an hourglass in her hand.
She turned it from man to woman
explaining that the heroes who'd saved
the day with Golden Fleeces, fought minotaurs
and joked in wooden horses had got it wrong.
They weren't supposed to fight and kill.
They weren't supposed to kill because of women.
That was a cop out. Passing the blame. Unfairly.
But then she said *what's fair?* and in the clouds
she showed me would-be heroines
growing up, facing life's wars and deceits,
practicing liberal philosophies, an existential movement,
a backlash to political patriarchs, undoing
the influences on behaviour of societal structures.

*What would the shape of the world look like
under heroines emanating from chaos
with visions of unity for earth?*
she said to someone over my shoulder.
(She couldn't be talking to me.
A Cassandra in my Italian family).
I sat at her feet to listen and took the cigarette she
handed me.

I saw the Devil take the east road to France, Germany,
Russia, and onwards to Egypt, Iraq, Iran, Vietnam and
Korea, all the way around to Kerak and Jerusalem,
and further back, my head was spinning with the
maimed bodies of the dead.
I was cold. The sun struggled in the smoke,
I heard soothsayers proclaim the end of the world.
Well? There was nothing I could say.
Suggesting religion wouldn't help. I'd seen
the Crusades, the Inquisition and Holocaust. I shrugged.
*Should our would-be heroines enter the debate or ought
Zeus wipe out humanity and let Hera lead instead?*
"You're the oracle," I said. "You tell me."

The Extra Chamber of my Heart
Aislinn Batstone

Sarah and I wait in the queue to the full body scanner that stands between us and the departure gates. There are six people in front of me. Five, then Hadley, then me and then Sarah.

Hadley's tang of sweat and soap reaches me. I sway closer, magnetised like when they placed us side by side in the fruit rows. That first night we stayed up late, exhausted from the work, talking, laughing, kissing—nothing more.

Now I breathe deeply to control the dreadful pounding of my heart. I focus on his hair, dreadlocks snaking with the movements of his head. Coloured beads in the centre of his back knock gently together, shifting sideways. I look up. He has turned, and my breath hitches as his gentle smile stabs at my chest. I stare at the floor.

This plane will fly back to our parents. Sarah and I will start college soon, and after six weeks working here, our bank accounts will look healthy. Summer is over, and we have hauled a crop of organic berries for those who can afford them.

There's a reason why my stomach fizzes like a wasp's nest as we inch our way towards the scanner blocking our exit. Authentic Organics has a monopoly on insect-pollinated food. Seasonal fruit pickers are young and are supposed to be politically naïve, but they don't trust us very much, and nothing of value should be taken from here.

Certainly not the robotic bee I have stored in the extra chamber of my heart.

Its solar charge has long since died, but still I imagine the whirring of its wings, a high uniform buzz in my chest, counterpoint to the beating of my heart, sister to the churning of my gut.

We found many birds lifeless in the rows this season, and one day Sarah opened a dead bird's chest with a fine scalpel from the frame of her titanium spectacles. There was a bee inside the bird's stomach, a robot bee, indigestible, an obstruction.

The birds die because the bees are so realistic, their appearance and behaviour indistinguishable from true insects; thus are the crops pollinated. The robots are cheap to make, cheap to break, but the secret of them is worth fields of gold, and they have never been taken outside the farm compound. Until now.

There are five people in front of me. Four, then Hadley, then me and then Sarah. Hadley is a scholarship boy; the other kids call him 'powder-eater' because powders have nourished him most of his life. Sarah's parents are doctors and she is as white as a cotton-ball cloud; her hair golden like the sun, her eyes blue like a morning sky. I am brown as a handful of earth, my eyes black like pebbles. I am brown as the miniature doll Hadley carved from a piece of apple-wood. He has still not seen me naked, but he got my breasts just right, high and pointed like teacups. He wears the carving on a leather strap around his neck.

Hadley isn't accustomed to the sweet fruit I sneaked into his mouth when the row supervisor looked away. Hadley's teeth are bad and his skin should shine like mine, but instead it is patchy and he stoops; his bones break easily. Authentic Organics thought he would be grateful for his chance to join us, we children of the upper middle classes. They hired him as a public relations exercise. And, in fact, Hadley was grateful. It was I who burned with rage for him.

There are four people in front of me. Three, then Hadley, then me and then Sarah.

Sarah cut me open one night in our bedroom, through my brown skin, which is real—it bleeds—and she opened my sternum by its hinges. Her forehead dripping sweat (my imagination, I was asleep) she opened the extra chamber of my heart and enclosed the bee like a keepsake in a locket.

She had given me two pills from a container of Altoids, visually identical to the mints. They put me to sleep, and when I woke in the morning, my chest felt crushed as if by a truckload of gravel, but I dared not take more painkillers or I would be too groggy to pick berries.

As it was, the field supervisor asked me what was wrong, and I told him I was menstruating. Even then I had to pretend to be only mildly affected, as I had made a statement as to my health, and that neither my artificial heart nor any other condition would affect my ability to do physical labour.

There are three people in front of me. Two, then

Hadley, then me and then Sarah.

When–if–we get back to Boston, Sarah's mother will check my wound, which has not healed well, and she will open my chest and remove the bee. My mother and father will study the creature and recreate it as best they can. Our dream is for hives to be created in orchards and fields across the country, for the monopoly of Authentic Organics to be broken.

The company did not know that I was raised for this. Where I grew up, when I looked to the left along my street, I saw the store that sells whole foods only the rich can afford. Over that way are healthy people who live in large, comfortable houses. But when I looked downhill to the right, to the cheap tall buildings over the train line, I saw spindly children with skin problems like Hadley's. My parents first showed me this contrast and taught me the source of the injustice as early as I could listen. They never allowed me to blame the poor for their own misfortunes. If my parents had been cleaners or shop workers, I would have died from the heart condition I was born with. This was never forgotten.

There are two people in front of me. One, then Hadley, then me and then Sarah.

The wound pained me badly for days afterwards, and though I grew closer to Hadley, I couldn't let him see. I could not risk what we were trying to achieve. That is why he has carved my breasts without seeing them, why there is gentle hurt in his eyes when he looks at me; he is asking 'why?' We talked for many hours about justice, we talked about everything except what was in my heart, and we touched each other in every way but the way we wanted to touch.

There is one person in front of me. Hadley.

My armpits slide against my sides with a sweat of horror and fear. If they catch Sarah and me, we will not be allowed to fly home. The secrets of the bees will remain inside the compound, inside the hive, inside the stomachs of dead birds. The children of the poor will continue to sicken and die. Perhaps the poor will die out. Is that what Authentic Organics wants? Do the rich not wonder who then will clean their houses? Who will work in their shops?

We do not know the punishment for someone who attempts to smuggle information from the compound. Authentic Organics may prosecute, or there may be some quiet and terrible consequence.

Hadley passes through the gate and waits smiling for me on the other side. The guards are not smiling; they are stone-faced. Lights flash and an alarm shrieks. Gloved hands clamp Hadley's shoulders, swivelling him roughly back the way he came. Hadley's eyes widen, they dart wildly before fixing on me. He reads something in my face and he understands. He is hurt, angry.

He meets my eyes with a hard steady gaze and touches his hand to the carving he wears around his neck. Does he sense its altered weight? He shouldn't; the chip embedded by Sarah is too light for a human touch.

We brought the chip with us to use only if we saw signs that Authentic Organics had heard rumours of a security breach. Unfortunately, by the time we saw those signs, the only one close enough was Hadley. He was touched that I wanted to sleep with the carving last night. Of course, he is also the perfect suspect. He understands this, I can see. From that, I feel like I will die.

They take him away.

I focus on the gate in front of me. If I enclose Hadley in my heart and build a chamber around him, perhaps I can step through the gate without revealing myself. The uncontrollable feelings can be controlled, I can do it if I just step this way. There are fewer guards by the gate, guards with less seniority—at least for now. The others have begun to deal with Hadley, pleased to have concrete evidence of a breach.

The sensor passes up and down my body. Lights flash. Two guards consult two screens and they shrug and nod and gesture me through. They have detected no change in the complex operations of my heart. The guards' inexperience must truly have worked in our favour, because it seems to me that my heart is shattered and forcing its way outwards through the raw part of my chest. Pain steals my breath. My mind plays Hadley's face, bright with pleasure one moment, distorted by fear in the next.

Sarah joins me and we walk to the departure gate. I do not look back. Our cause will take a giant leap forward, thousands of people will benefit and I, of all people, should know that broken hearts can be mended. The greater good must be put ahead of the good of any individual. I must not think about what might happen to Hadley, and I will try to recall his face happy and bright, not shocked and afraid, or angry and hurt.

Sarah and I board the plane and take our seats. I clip on my seatbelt, sit back to await take-off, and all at once the sequence of events replays itself in my mind. Again and again his face shifts as he registers my betrayal.

I cannot turn my thoughts away. I am trapped, imprisoned like the bee, wings flailing against the walls of this enclosure. Could there have been another way to save all those others who are not him? I think I must be dying, dying from what was left unsaid, dying from the fact of what I have done, dying from the price of the secret contained in the extra chamber of my heart.

Requiem for Vali*
Jaya Penelope

You were Our Lady of Sorrows
a dream in a dark place
a cave of gilded bones.
 You were Our Lady of Claws, of Talons
Our Lady of Teeth and Fur, but oh
your feet, how sweet their jig
on cobbled streets.

You spoke in fox-tongue
met creatures halfway to their wildness
it was the human tongue that hung
heavy, dumb in your mouth.

You'll have a paradise
all your own, Lady, some wild
frill-skirted place, like your mountain
valley in Italy, where the eels snake
their heads out of the river
for you to stroke
and a pack of dogs nuzzle
your blood-hemmed skirts.

Where your wild fox curls
again, a bushfire in the jewelled
bed of your heart. There your baroque
breasts weep dove eggs to feed
your fierce family, and a procession
of bowed young men carry water
up mountain paths for you to drink.

Now, you watch over the world
in your pantaloons, your dancing slippers
The cobalt blue humming bird
rises again and again
from the henna flame
of your hair.

---

* *Vali Myers, Australian born painter, dancer & lover of wild creatures died in Melbourne in 2003.*

The Fisherman and the Cormorant
Therese Doherty

It was better this way. To have supple wings instead of arms, and dark as night feathers covering my skin. To be able to dive deep down into the brownish-blue below, to fly amongst water weeds and catch fish in my bill.

He didn't know when he flung his curse that I would thank him for changing me. He had wanted me, the old leer-eyed lech; and wanted to grow his own power by stealing from mine. When I refused him, showed him that my womanly wisdom was so much more than his, he feared me, as men so often fear women. Now, blinded by sour jealousy, by bitter contempt, he wanted nothing but revenge.

He struck me with his wand carved with magic symbols, and bellowed hateful spell-words, and at first, I was horrified and in terrible pain. My body shrank and narrowed and my neck stretched out long and lithe; I grew clumsy webbed feet and a clacking bill; and my hands, perhaps the one thing I do miss, were no longer able to touch or hold, as they stretched out and fledged and I became winged.

Changing is always a difficult undertaking. We avoid it more often than we embrace it. But I had no choice in the matter. Frightened, and still in some agony, I did all I could do at the time: I flew away.

It was in my flight that I looked down at the earth below me, and I suppose you could say I gained a new perspective on my predicament. It didn't take me long, no more than a wingbeat or two, to accept my new body, for I could fly! — and don't we all dream of that? In flight I was free, free as no human could ever be. So I flew away from the vengeful he-witch who had turned me, and I wholeheartedly adopted my new form.

After some time in the air, when I knew I was safe, I smelt cold, welcoming water on the wind, and came to rest at a lake. There, I set about learning to swim, flying underwater like a black comet; and there were plenty of frogs and silvery fish to eat, so I was more than content. Indeed, I came to love my sleek new body, my glossy feathers, my bright blue-green eyes, more than I had ever loved myself as a woman.

I would sometimes sit on a rock by the water,

drying my lovely, green-tinged wings, and think of people, remembering them always doing doing doing, as if their lives depended on it. As a bird I knew better, for being is so much more satisfying, so much more delightful and virtuous. When the elders had said that the animals, in their wildness, were wiser and worthier than humans, they spoke the elemental truth. I knew this because I felt it, in my hollow bones and bird-flesh and right to the tips of my feathers. I was air and water, earth too, and fire was in my heart. I dwelt joyously by my lake. Simply being. Being cormorant.

Though on the night of the first new moon, when starlight was all there was to see by, I changed back. I had just got cosy in my night time roost, when I was overcome by a keen-edged pain, and I fell from my perch to the ground, writhing and crying out. Arms and legs burst from my bird limbs, my graceful neck receded, my gleaming feathers recoiled, and my pointed bill shrank back to smooth, wide lips. After my few weeks in bird-form, I lay in shock, confused by my huge size, my great soft and gangling body.

This, then, was the curse: to be animal, yet not wholly so. To be turned back, excruciatingly, every dark of the moon, so I was neither one thing nor the other. Torn from the bliss of being, and shackled to doing once more, a mere human. It was only for one night, each turn of the moon, but it was still too much. I would spend those long nights longing for my bird body, shivering with the cold on my bare, goosebumped skin. A woman alone, dreaming only of fish and flight.

This was my life. Mostly bird, but woman too.

Then one day a man arrived on the shore of the lake. A man with sad eyes and a sweet, humble face, carrying a swag and dragging a little canoe. He set up camp in a sandy clearing where the ground was ridged with tree roots, and made a little shack for shelter from the rain beside a golden-flowered banksia tree. Lighting a fire to warm himself, he sat staring into the flames, looking forlorn.

The sun soon set on that beguiling scene, and the smell of smoke from the campfire lingered in the air all night.

The next morning the man sat on a stone by the water's edge, like a shag on a rock, watching the sunlight igniting the shallows, rippling them with flares of gold. Later, he paddled out in his canoe, slow and steady, handmade fishing rod in his fist, and I saw him catch a brown trout. He killed it dead, quick, hitting it over the head, and it slid with a wet slap onto the floor of the canoe. With head bowed for a time, as if in a posture of grief or reverence, the man sat with his elbows resting on his knees, his hands hanging limply, a tear in his eye. Then he slowly paddled back to the shore.

The smell of cooking trout drifted over that evening, and for a moment, just one bird-flown moment, I wanted my human form again, so I could taste it. Mild and slightly greasy in my mouth, chewed between two rows of white teeth. Then I caught a fish and swallowed it whole, raw, straight down my gullet, with a gratified snap.

It seemed the man had come to stay at my lake, and I wasn't sure how I felt about this, to have a human so close by, so tempting and repelling. I was cautious, but curious too.

Each day I swam closer and closer, popping up near his canoe, and watching his shy face. Sometimes he would look down into the water, as if he could see right to the bottom, into the green and weedy deepness, and I wondered what he saw there, this human with his limited human eyes.

He saw me, eventually. My streamlined, sheeny body, my azure eyes that saw through water and air. He did not speak, but smiled, and watched, and wondered. He did not need to say I was beautiful, for I knew it already.

Then the moon hid once more, on a dark, overcast night, and I could not help crying out, whimpering as I transformed and trembled on the cold ground. And he came through the blackness, the sweet-faced man, with concern and awe resonant in his breathing. He lifted me, carried me in his strong human arms, back to the camp, laying me gently in his shack. He said not a word, but breathed out softly, and slept, invisible by my side.

That night I wasn't cold or alone.

Though before the blush of dawn I left him, with a whisper of thanks, a shriek and a soft splash, as I changed back and entered the water. From the lake's cool centre I saw him on the shore, poor bewildered man, wondering if he had been dreaming.

That day I swam to him as he fished, darting around and under the canoe, a black shooting star in an upside-down sky. He was silent, as ever; but we animals know that language is so much more than just words. His sweet face and his sad eyes and his man's body, all said, Come, my dear little cormorant, my black water-raven. Come, catch me a fish.

So I did. I caught him a glistening, wriggling silver fish, and he took it from my bill, dispatched its water-full life with tenderness, and gazed quizzically into my vivid avian eyes.

He knew me then.

That night we dreamed—the man in his shack and me in my tree. We dreamed of a grey fishwife, with a dillybag full of moon-bright fish, and waterweed in her grizzly hair. The old woman said there was a way to break the spell, to make me changeless once more.

'Take cormorant-caught fish,' she said, with a glance at me, 'and skin them without tearing. Smoke the skins dry, and sew them together with fishbone needle and fish-gut thread. Make a fish-skin blanket, and speak not a word until it is done. Then,' she said, with a cock of her head to him, 'throw it over your love.'

So I caught fish for him, I did. I sped through the water like an aquatic acrobat, seizing my slippery prey. He cut away their flashing skins with a skilled hand, and hung them over a low, smokey fire, before piercing the skins with his fine bone needle, joining them seam to seam.

By the next new moon the blanket was half-made, and I came to his camp when I changed, spent the dark night with him, warm skin against skin, my hands taking their fill of touch. Man and woman. All too human.

This is how we were—a fisherman and a cormorant, a human and a bird—making a magic fish-skin blanket, together. To break a spell.

Then the moon changed again, in her unceasing round, hid her face anew; the blanket was finally finished, and I came to him in woman-form once more. That night was joyous, expectant, all cares laid aside. But before daybreak, he took the blanket in his hands, smoke-smelling and fish-sweet, and spoke his first and only words to me: 'Will you stay?'

It pained me, then, his soft-hearted humanness, his confusion about the curse. In the growing grey light, the bird in me shook my head, resolute, for I was done with doing, though the woman did so with regret. He nodded, acceptant, bowing to my bird-wish, sorrowful and silent. He let the blanket, all our weeks of work, drop heavily by his side. Had it all been for nothing?

And then the sun's light broke free of the horizon and I began to change, right before his sad, human eyes. To shrink and lengthen and fledge, until I was small and black and beautiful. I flapped my wings, turned my head on its long, graceful neck, and he remembered what the fishwife had said. *Throw it over your love.*

Picking up the fish-skin blanket, he took me gently in his arms, held me close to his fluttering heart, and cast the magic blanket around us both. Then we beat our gleaming wings as one, and dived down deep.

Midnight, Siren, & Fire
Kathryn Lyster

midnight

I went into the orchard
   alone,   needing
to speak to the trees
   seeking their quiet
   steady
   counsel
   sound of sap rising
   of leaves pushing
   through stems
   of hidden
   unspoken
   green   fruit
   being dreamed
i went with my head bowed
   ears   alert
     the fox cub
 at my heels,
   her black-tipped tail
    slipping neatly
  through   undergrowth
i knew what the pear
     trees   would say
that's why i'd stayed   away
   clinging to your
   skin
   like it was mine,
   clutching
   your chest hair
   for survival
the trees told me
    to let go
 to surrender you
   back to the night
   give you up.
the fox,   little face tilted
     to the pale autumn
   moon
  agreed.

                                       (my fingers uncurled)

siren

After the night –
  morning mist rising
     i watch you
  through windows
closed against
  damp
your strong hands
part   dark trees
  ache
 between my thighs
i imagine
     you
  at   lake's
edge
  water waiting
to   swallow
   you   whole
skin   lit up
   syrup dream
light
  sleepy dragonflies
    drone   reeds
bend   to lick your
        edges
  below the surface
her   silver tail
   flashes   ripples
 spool   from
   black ink   hair
     if you swim deep
    she'll have   you

the water   my sister   our love.

fire

Walls   alive with
  darting flames
    eating the edges
 gnawing the skeleton
   of wood
 from the pear
     tree
felled by   wind
  you weren't there
to chop + carry
  i did it all on my own
                snow
the house,   a bunker
  a   sorrow-storer
   my hands   weave
a basket without
 my mind
 push straw
 into braids
  and   wind
 circles of time
fox   stirs   fur   hot
   against my shins

Muffled   sound
at the door
    low growl,
   an animal
    fox's russet shackles
rise   fire brightens
  i take a burning log
     listen,
breathless
  against the heavy oak
    there is no lock
  i always had you
    a whimper,
   pained
i open up
 a wolf,
    grey female
    ancient
    faded muzzle

          a fleshless-thing
      fox runs for cover
i let the wolf in
      she limps to the
   hearth
         droops down
      heaves her tired
   bones   lies
                listless
               sighs
    fox's scared eyes burn
i   give them both a
    knot of soup-soaked
          bread
         two tongues
             against my hands
pull my red cloak around me
   and sing.

The Menkas
Tamara Lazaroff

Not that long ago, in Macedonia, there was a man. He lived in a small town on a cobbled street in a wooden house. In it, he had a wife and a bear. He also had a job – not in the house, but at the metal smelter in the town's centre. It was this or nothing else. So, it was unfortunate, then, that the products and byproducts from the metal smelter contaminated and poisoned the town's river, air and earth.

But that is a whole other story.

The point is that the man had the wife, and he had the bear. And both of their names were Menka.

The first, his wife, had always been a Menka, ever since the man had known her. She was his valentine-faced childhood sweetheart. They had just been married.

The bear, on the other hand, still a cub, had been nameless, as far as the man knew, when he'd first found it in the forest in the surrounding mountains not long after the honeymoon. Then, it had seemed abandoned, so he'd picked it up and taken it home and called it Menka, too, because it was a girl. And because, even though he could sometimes be serious, he very much liked a joke. And this was a very good joke, he thought. To have two Menkas – one for a wife, and one for a bear. A great, great joke.

His friends thought so, too. Hilarious! The friends who also worked at the metal smelter. The same ones who every Friday night went over to the man's wooden house to play cards, and bluff and bet, and lose and win, and laugh and shout and swear. This they did each time with high, high spirits. And so, of course, eventually, inevitably, at some point in the evening they'd all get hungry and thirsty. Then the man would call out, 'Oh, Menka! Oh, Menka! Bring us some pretzels and peanuts and beer.'

And Menka would come – one or the other. But which? The man could never be sure. Sometimes it was Menka the wife who'd push through the door wearing a thin, worn smile across her no longer valentine face. At other times it was Menka the bear, still a cub but growing, who'd lumber in on her hind legs carrying the pretzels and the peanuts and the beer on the silver tray that had been a wedding gift.

When that happened the man's friends would laugh and laugh. They'd slap each other on the back, fold in half at their middles, wipe the tears from their eyes and say, 'Oh, brother, what a good joke. A great joke. Really, it's the very, very best.'

Then, eventually, inevitably, when it was late and the games were over the friends would have to leave. They'd go back home to their wives – if they had them – or to their mothers who still washed their socks and boiled their eggs. But none went home to a bear.

And so, life carried on as it always did in its seemingly small, ordinary way. Weeks, months, years went by and Menka the wife's marriage to the man matured in its way. As could be expected, Menka the bear cub grew, too, as bears will tend to do. The men went to work at the metal smelter. They didn't like it, but what else could they do?

It, the metal smelter and its products and byproducts, unfortunately, continued to poison and pollute the town's river, air and earth. A chemical spill here, a chemical spill there, no one seemed to notice or care. Again, that is a whole other story.

The point is that Friday night card nights, they always rolled around. And each time they did, it could be guaranteed, it could be relied upon one hundred percent, that at some point in the evening the man and his friends would get hungry and thirsty. Then the man – he always did – would call out, 'Oh, Menka! Oh, Menka! Bring us some pretzels and peanuts and beer.'

And Menka would come. But which? Which one? That joke never grew thin.

If it was Menka the bear who came lumbering in, the men, without fail, without fail, would slap each other on their backs. Their sides would split open. Their guts would hang out and stain the seat of their pants. Oh, how they'd laugh and laugh. But why exactly it was they did laugh not the man nor his friends could've said, if they'd been asked. But nobody did ask. So they didn't have to say.

All the friends had to do, when it was late, once the games were over, was go home to their wives or their mothers, but none to a bear. And the man, all he had to do, was climb the creaky stairs to the bed where Menka the wife lay. Once there, then all he had to do was pull off his pants and shirt down to his boxers and socks and lean over and whisper into his wife's ear, 'Oh, Menka. Oh, Menka. Are you awake?' hoping to get some loving. And sometimes he would and sometimes – increasingly – he wouldn't.

Like this, life went on seemingly ordinarily, until one cold winter's night. It was a Friday. Card night as usual. Everything the same. The bluffs, the bets. The losses, the wins. The laughs, the hunger, the thirst. It was late. It had become so. The games were done. The man's friends had just left. And as usual, the man, a little drunk, but not too much, was beginning his ascent of the creaky stairs to where he supposed Menka the wife – why wouldn't she? she always had – would be lying in their bed.

He climbed and climbed, wobbling as he went. Even so, still he was confident. He took it for granted, the way things would work out. But when he reached the door to the room that they shared, he opened it to find, to his shock, his surprise, that no Menka did lie in the place she should have – though the covers on her side had been pulled down – and the lamp had been left on. It shone, and the window had been opened wide. Why? He did not know.

'Menka?' the man asked, quietly, almost to himself as he looked towards the window to see that outside it, snow, the first of the season, fell. Light and white it made no sound. Falling. Snow. Outside the open window.

But the man did not bother to close it, that window. The cold, he didn't seem to feel it. Instead, by the light of the lamp, he pulled off his shirt and pants down to his boxers and socks. And then he pulled down the covers and got into his side of the bed, thinking that Menka, his wife, would be along any moment. But she wasn't.

And so, after some time had passed – too much of it as far as he was concerned – the man called out, 'Oh, Menka! Oh, Menka! Where are you? Come keep me warm!'

Then, quickly, he turned off the lamp. He'd never done that before. And he waited. And he wondered – but which one? – which Menka would come? Of the answer he could not be sure.

In anticipation, his heart beat a little faster in his

chest. Excitement made his blood pump triple-time through his veins. Giddy with desire, he congratulated himself. Now this, this, having two Menkas, one for a wife and one for a bear, was not just a good, great joke that he could not have explained even if he'd wanted to. It was a thrill, a chance, a risk. Like bluffs and bets, or losses and wins. Like playing cards on Friday nights, but much, much better. In the dark, he waited as, outside the open window, snow, the first of the season, fell.

And soon, soon Menka – but which one? which one? – did come. She was coming. The man could hear her footsteps climbing up the creaky stairs. And then there was the bedroom door clicking open and closed. The man heard that, too. Then there was the weight of her, of Menka – but which one? which one? – on the bed as she sat and then lay.

The man's heart beat faster still.

What a thrill, what a thrill.

And he reached out to the Menka, to whichever one she was. In the dark, he drew that Menka close. He caressed her skin – or was it fur? But how soft it was. He kissed her lips, her open mouth. But what sharp teeth she had that bit at him. Ouch. And how warm her body that received him. And how low the growl in his ear. And how sharp the nails that clawed down his back. And how strong the thighs that gripped him tight, tighter.

'Oh! Menka! Oh! Menka!' the man cried out.

And then it was all over.

The man lay flat on his back. He gasped for air. He took great gulps of it, saying over and over again the same, 'Oh, Menka. Oh, Menka. That was amazing, that was amazing.'

But Menka – still, which one? – said nothing.

'Menka?' said the man.

What had he done?

'Menka, my wife,' he begged, 'speak to me.'

But Menka would not.

And so, even though he would rather have rolled over and slept and woken to another ordinary day, something in him – curiosity? courage? shame? – made him reach over and turn on the light of the lamp to look the truth square in the face. He was prepared.

But there beside him on the bed, under the

cover and on the sheet, was only Menka the wife, his childhood sweetheart with her once again valentine face. Drowsily, she smiled at him. She stretched her arms above her head. She yawned long and loud. Ah! That was the sound she made. But, still, she did not speak.

It didn't matter. The man, overwhelmed with relief, kissed her nose – 'Oh, Menka!' – he kissed her eyes – 'Oh, Menka' – he kissed her cheeks. He wept and said, 'I'm so happy to see you. You see, I, I, I thought… I, I, I hoped… I, I, I feared…'

Menka the wife, the woman, only put a finger to her husband's lips to shush him, his stuttering, his stammering. And then, and only then, did she do a strange and out-of-the-ordinary thing.

She closed her eyes. She squeezed their lids as if to gather her energy, resolve and will. And then, when she opened them again – wide and bright, they sparked with life – she took one great leap and landed to stand, naked, before her husband, on her feet, on the rug, at the foot of the bed.

There she said, 'Well, tell me, my husband. What was it? What did you think and hope and fear? I wonder. Could it have been this?' she said as she proceeded to unzip the zip of her skin-suit that began at the top of her head and ended at a place between her legs – to reveal – Menka the bear.

Menka the bear! How could it be? How could it be?

The man's jaw hung slack. His eyes blinked in his head. And the back of his throat went dry, horribly. There was no way he could answer the questions that were being posed to him.

'Or was it this? Was it? Tell me, my husband. Is this what you thought or hoped or feared?' said Menka the bear in the voice of the Menka the wife – it really was very confusing – as she quickly, expertly, as if she'd done it a thousand times before, proceeded to unzip her fur-suit which began at a place at the top of her bear head and ended at a place between her bear legs – to reveal – another Menka altogether, of sorts.
And then that Menka unzipped and revealed.
And that Menka unzipped and revealed, too.
As did the next, and the next, and the next.
Too many Menkas zipped out of and into every kind of

suit or skin or get-up or costume imaginable and unimaginable, both.

These Menkas, they also did something else. It was only logical, even the man thought so himself. With each unzip and each reveal, they got smaller and smaller still – as with Russian *babushka* dolls – until standing before the man on the rug at the foot of the bed was the very last Menka. Tiny, a speck, a wisp.

And she, too, said, in her tiny Menka voice, just as every Menka before her had, 'Well, well, my husband. Tell me. Tell me, please. Is this what you thought or hoped for or feared?' as she too unzipped – and revealed – nothing.

Nothing.

There was no Menka left. There were no Menkas anymore. Just the pileup of suits and skins and get-ups and costumes. But they too – bang – woof – poof – went up, spontaneously, dramatically, in a flash and a puff of smoke. And that was that.

And though the man tried to find her that night and on the many that followed, under the rug, in the fridge, out on the cobbled street, running, running, calling her name, he never did. The wife, the bear and every-Menka else were never heard of or seen again.

So, life went on – it had to – it always did. Seasons came and went, years. The man matured in his way. Inevitably, eventually, he wrinkled, he sagged, he moaned, he ached. Even so, he still went to work at the metal smelter, along with the other men, his friends, until one day, unexpectedly, it was boarded up and closed down and marked with signs saying DANGER! TOXIC! STAY OUT! But, once again, that is a whole other story.

Only Friday night card nights remained. It was just that now the man and his friends had to get their own pretzels and peanuts and beer. But that wasn't that hard. They got used to it. Harder was finding something to laugh about. Instead, they became philosophical.

'Brother,' said the friends to the man. 'Things can only get better. There's talk the Germans will be opening up a new factory in town soon. Still, even so, no matter what happens, it's not good to be alone. You should find a new wife. You really should.'

But the man only shrugged his shoulders and, poker-faced, looked at the hand he'd been dealt.

Without saying a thing, he shrugged his shoulders one more time and laid his hopeful, reckless bet.

Lilith
Gail Willems

the clock strikes twelve
small death of night
seconds shiver
your fingers hook in my palm
tined by strings
that thrum the space between us
take your eyes from your hands
drown them
in the long soft ache of chianti tears

II

my mouth a double kiss
breath a ghost
lips of night and shadow
whisky peat eyes
a labyrinth of promises
weight of lust tangles my hair
look in the mirror
my shadow at your shoulder
ripples of voice
like ice on a hot stove
melts into your soul
remembers my touch

rake out the cracks
read the story
where love fell through

Bits and Bolts and Blood
Louise Pieper

The greenwoods rustle and seethe with the beasts and faeries who steal human children. You don't need to stray from the path. Venture alone and they charm and mislead you, beguile and snatch you, and before the basket you drop rolls to rest, their teeth meet in your soft, soft flesh, their caps soak up your red, red blood and you're lost to the world forever. So my grandmother says. So everyone knows.

Foolish towns, like Kelston, turn their back on the greenwoods, but the woods don't ignore them in return. The trees encroach. They sidle up, limbs touching limbs, reaching to tap at windows and walls. 'Here we are,' their scratching reminds the townsfolk. Deep and dark. Dangerous. And, after a storm, damp and dripping.

The tree which reaches, from the greenwoods to the inn, is slippery as a sleep-tickled trout. Strange, given the pinwood's affinity for truth. I balance on the rain-slick bough; arms wide, elbows bent, like some gawky village girl, trembling to weave into the dance. Like the Knave of Bolts, fool that he is, poised at the precipice. A trickle of sweat traces the knobs of my spine.

What would Zouza say about a slippery tree of truth? I let my grandmother's papery voice rustle rich words in my head.

Contradictory. Incongruous. Oppugnant. Not capricious like you, wilful Redchen.

The syllables rattle like dice in the cup of my skull. Even in my thoughts she scolds me. Soothes me. When I lie awake at night, her dry murmur and the rasp of the cards are lullabies to drop me into the cool depths of sleep. When I lose patience with tasks the village children have long since mastered, her words calm my snarled rage.

Fortitude. Tenacity. Valour. All things have their season, Redchen.

Truth–it's not my season for obedience. I've seen fourteen winters and though Zouza ties me with words and affection, I chaff at the leash, yearning for something I can't name. She hopes this journey will ease my restlessness and so it might, if she will only tell me the truth of why we've come.

Is it a vow-taking which calls for her skills – some alliance in business or marriage which won't proceed until its luck's been told? Are we in Kelston to trace a child taken by faeries and a changeling creature left in its place? Zouza can tease the truth from her cards and tell the parents how to win back their child. Or is it a lost treasure or inheritance which requires a luck-teller's skill?

Zouza won't tell me. She nurses her secrets and I rebel.

She told me to wait on the balcony, so I put aside my boots and my promises and slipped into the trees. Capricious? Oh, I'm that; and contrary and wilful and wild. My boots lie where I left them, lumpen as mud-caked potatoes. Their iron hob-nails glisten wet and black.

Always wear them, Zouza said. But who can climb in heavy boots?

My toes flex, as I slide forward. The tree was less than a span from the balustrade, when I climbed out. Coming back, it hangs sullen with the weight of the rain. My feet lick the buttery bark, but they can't taste the truth of the wood beneath. I bend my knees, spine straight, and coax a bounce from the bough. Rain drips in my eyes as I judge the distance. I beg the Beast of Bits to grant me wings, or at least success. Droplets scatter as I throw myself forward.

I crash into the rail, one arm pinned and the other flung over it. My ribs howl protest, as my cap slides over one eye. The cobbles, three floors below, reach for me. They crave my embrace, which the balcony spurns. I scrabble, bruising my knees. I kick and kick again. Slip, and have no breath to scream. My toe stubs the top of a carved support and grips like a leech.

Legs straining, arms weak as dough, I heave and tilt myself over the rail. I hang there, like a poor trembling trout gasping the air. My hips ache, with my skirts bunched beneath them, half-tucked into an old pair of breeches, but I can't move for thinking of those mud-streaked cobbles. What good has disobedience done me? If I'd waited on the balcony until Zouza's telling was done, I wouldn't be wet and scraped and bruised. I squirm forward until my hands reach the floor.

Refractory. Obstreperous. Incorrigible.

My nostrils flare. If Zouza were luck-telling the room would be shut. The curtains are drawn, but the doors creak in the rain-scudding breeze and waft a scent to me. Not beeswax and tangen oil, to boast the room is recently cleaned. Not cloves and smoke, which clings to Zouza, especially when she's told someone's luck. It's the scent of Blotgyre Day, when beasts are slaughtered for the winter. It's the iron-harsh reek of spilled blood.

My feet strike the stone, my hand snatches the door, my mouth cries, "Zouza!"

She'd scold me, caution me, tell me to slow down, use my head, stay calm; but I'm already in the room, blinking against the dimness, and Zouza will never tell me anything again. A sound escapes my lips, like the cry of a wounded fox. My legs fail me and I fall hard. My cap tumbles to the floor, followed by long, lank hair which curtains my face. Not enough to block the sight of Zouza. She sprawls on the floor, arms flung wide, and cards scattered, with her life-blood pooled beneath her.

Something in the room growls. It takes too long to realise it's me. The hand I reach towards her drips scarlet tears and my guts twist. Zouza's blood is everywhere, spattered on her dark dress, her darker skin. Her hair, once raven black, then woven with silver strands, is now streaked with gore. I break into a sweat. All that blood, thick with her secrets. I whimper as part of me dies; maybe it's the child I can't be without her.

Think, Redchen, think – Zouza would say – *bottle the fear, the pain, the scream that taps at the back of your teeth. Think first, feel later, when you're safe.*

I drag my gaze from the gaping mess of her throat and follow the line of her sleeve to her palm, so much paler than her old, polished-teak skin. Pale, but not as pale as my fish-belly flesh. I shudder. In her right hand she holds the Knave of Bolts. The Apprentice – expiation. The Fool, she says, when I've displeased her. It's my card, my signifier, just as the Crown of Bolts is hers. The Crone – wisdom.

The cards love her, they come to her hand. Did she call it, as she died? Did she think of me? The rest of the deck is scattered–the Nine of Bolts on Zouza's chest, the Book of Bits in the folds of her skirt, the Beast of

Blood pinned by her outflung left hand.

Betrayal. Reward. Strength.

My gaze follows the line of her arm to the heavy wooden cabinet against the wall. Rugs, bags and books spill on the floor, as if it heaved up its contents at the sight of Zouza's death. But, no. Someone has searched the room with violent disregard for our possessions.

Truth – they call to me.

Zouza's dice and cards usually lie in her pinwood box. For our journey she left the box under the bed in her cottage and brought them in a black silk bag. It's hidden in the shadows beneath the cabinet. I know it's there, from the scent of the dice.

A solid gold die for Bits, it is cold and heavy as the crimes some would commit for its worth. *Avarice.*

A red die, carved from bone, so it ought to be white, but it tells tales for the suit of Blood and Zouza fed it well. *Obligation.*

A black die for Bolts, carved from a lightning-struck pinwood tree. Truth in the wood and in the telling. *Acuity.*

They smell of chance, of luck which flashes like sunlight glancing off a tossed coin. They smell of power and of cloves and smoke. Of Zouza, for she kept them close and crooned to them. Some luck-tellers put themselves into their cards, but paper tears and burns and is lost. There are fifty-four cards, but only three dice, and it's the dice which refine the telling.

I scrabble across the floor in an awkward crouch, lie flat on my belly and reach for the bag. The tramp of feet, mounting the stairs of Kelston's second-finest inn, sounds through the wood beneath my ear. My fingers close on the silk cord as the floorboards pass on the stairs' gossip. Four pairs of feet. One, the inn wife, in fashionable heels which pinch her toes. Two, heavy but in step with each other. They've spent long hours learning that martial dance. The fourth pair skips, eager as debutantes. Cold iron rings at their heels, all but baying for the hunt. Jaeger.

I kiss the wood for its help and scramble to my feet, snatch my travel bag from amid the mess and slip the strap over my head. What will they think, to find me with Zouza dead and the dice in my hand? My gaze flicks to the Nine of Bolts – betrayal and murder. Quick, then. I stuff the dice, a blanket, a flask and a loaf of bread into my bag as I cross the room. I twist my hair and grab my cap from the floor. Only after I jam it onto my head do I realise it's wet with Zouza's blood. Red-handed and red-faced – any jaeger would condemn me on sight.

I hate to leave her so, but the steps beat on the final staircase. I lean down, lift the Knave of Bolts from her fingers and tuck it into my bag.

Oh, Grandmother, what cold hands you have.

Outside, the pinwood drips with the false promise of safety. I climb the rail, take a deep breath and leap to the bough. My knees, already bruised, jar again. I bite back a cry and struggle to my feet. In the room the inn wife screams. I bolt to the pinwood's core, scramble up and around, swallowing pain and curses. Iron spurs ring on the stone balcony as I press my back to the trunk. How can I outrun a jaeger?

They are the Erls' hunters–fleet as deer, vicious as stoats, clever and relentless as wolves. Bad luck for one to be in Kelston, to lay the blame for Zouza's death on her half-wild, half-witted apprentice – a girl who can neither scribe her letters, nor ply a needle. A girl at odds with cows and dogs and horses. Oh, I know what they whisper about me, in our village.

Fae-struck. Misbegot. Cursed.

Zouza tried to keep it from me, but the cards speak truth and so do flung stones.

What other secrets has Zouza carried with her into death? Who would kill her and why? Who'd risk the ill-luck of slaying a luck-teller? Such a blow and the way she fell… By the Book of Blood, I hope they were fool enough to attack her face on and she cursed them with her last breath. That would be justice.

My head pounds beneath my bloody cap and my heart bruises my ribs. I'm sure it can beat no faster, but it proves me wrong, leaping like a fly-bitten colt, as the jaeger sounds his horn. At the front of the inn, his pack howls their response. The Knave of Blood. The Jaeger–*passion*. All I know is terror. I risk one glance around the trunk. The jaeger stands firm as a dark tree, his russet coat flapping around his knees, eager as his hounds for the chase. He holds his horn to his lips. In his other hand, he has my boots. My scent. He'll hunt me.

He lowers the horn and I pinch my lips to

silence my gasp. I know him, or at least I saw him, years ago, in Zouza's cottage. He'd come to argue with her. He hadn't been a jaeger then – only young and lean and angry, clenching his hand around the hilt of the knife he'd worn at his hip. As dark as Zouza, his eyes had held none of her warmth.

"This whelp," he'd sneered at me, "is no blood of yours."

As if I'd not known. As if our skin didn't trumpet that truth. He'd called me worthless and worse. Zouza had shrugged.

"What's blood," she'd mused, "but payment or power. Same as bits. Same as bolts."

It was true enough. They were the three sources of power, the three kinds of commerce. *Blood. Gold. Magic.* The cards and dice reflect all of life in their telling.

"She's not Gretchen," he'd said.

Zouza's face had seemed carved of granite.

"You owe me this," she'd whispered through clenched teeth. "You let her die."

Had it been as much as ten years ago? No. I'd been old enough for Zouza to send me outside then – although I'd wanted to ask who Gretchen was, with a name so similar to mine – and I'd tied my own bootlaces, which I'd not learned to do until I'd seen eight winters. Six years, then. No more. As I'd closed the door, I'd seen the card Zouza toyed with. Sky of Blood. The Moon – *deception*. Had either of them spoken the truth?

I can't know and I can't spare the time to worry at it. I shake off the past, turn and run. For all my grandmother's warnings I'll take my chances with the woods, rather than face the judgement of the jaeger.

The trees hide me and soon enough night blankets me, but I don't know how to escape him and his hounds. I snatch at sleep, tucked in the embrace of conspiring trees and my dreams are harried by the Court of Blood, sharpening their knives. Vain hope, that they'd side with me against a jaeger.

Dawn finds me huddled in an oak. Two ravens perch nearby and I throw them a crust of bread, grateful that the King and Queen of Bolts watch over their Knave. For all their grim demeanour, I know their dark majesties don't mean death, but transformation and renewal. I need a new start, but to find the right path I must know the truth. And for that... I bow to the ravens. It's clear enough I must beat the jaeger to grandmother's house.

Zouza's voice echoes in my thoughts. *Three things, Redchen, my little red cap. Promise me. Always wear your boots outside. Be careful not to touch blood. And never touch my pinwood box.* Promises promised, but all to be broken. At least the third I can do with a clear conscience, for Zouza said I must take the box, with her dice and her cards, when she died. The cards are lost, but the pinwood holds the secrets she whispered to it and I need only touch its wood to know them.

I grind my teeth together, to try and still the ache which rose in them overnight and climb down the tree. From the lowest branch, I drop to the earth. The shock of it jars up through my bare feet. The ravens take to the air, shrieking. If I weren't hunted, I'd scream after them. A line of cold fire runs from my soles to my head. I bite my lip to hold in my cry and taste blood.

Calamity. Cataclysm. Pandemonium.

I crouch, shudder with the pain, and run my tongue over my teeth. They feel longer, sharper, more crowded. I've no time for this... this *anomalous dentition*. The taste of my blood spins my senses and I tear open my bag, to rinse my mouth with water from my flask. The full deck of Zouza's cards spill out. They've come to me, as so often they went to my grandmother's hand.

Full? I count them rapidly. Fifty-three. I fan them, but I don't need to search. I know which card is missing, know it in my bones. The Knave of Blood. The Jaeger. My head pounds as if fire binds my skull, rather than the cap Zouza felted for me. How can the Court of Blood defend such treachery? For certain he killed her and now hunts me, with the Erl's authority behind him. He'd put the blame for his crime on a friendless, foundling girl.

But why had he killed her? I clutch the cards and look down at the Crown of Blood. The Mother – *sacrifice*. I try to still my tumbled thoughts, to let the cards guide me.

What are the jaeger's intentions? I break the deck.

Seven of Bits – *personal gain*.

Oh, he wants Zouza's dice and her power, I

can't doubt it. What – I must know – what is wrong with me?

One of Bolts – *clarity*. A decision to let one see through deception.

What does it mean? I grimace, take a deep breath and ask again. What will I find at my grandmother's cottage?

I hope for the Beast of Bits. The Dragon – *victory*. Instead, it's the Book of Bolts, with its black-robed Magus, holding aloft a dark tome – *knowledge*.

Then I must go. I shake myself, as a dog will, and settle again in my skin. I tuck the cards away and turn north, where the trees grow close. *Inhospitable. Minacious. Direful.* If the jaeger doesn't want to lose his pack, or break his horse's leg, he'll keep to the paths. Not me. Not me.

My breath harvests the scent of flowers, moist leaves and rot. My feet caress and crush ferns and skeleton leaves as I run. I let the greenwoods fill my heart until there is no room left for Zouza's warnings. I'm not afraid of what I'll find. I climb trees and cross paths and wade through streams. The hounds bell to the south and I hope they've found the burrow where I buried my skirt to delay them. I hope the jaeger is distracted, waylaid and lost.

The woods sing to me and the sap in the trees stirs like slow blood. Birds, beasts, monsters, fae – all of the greenwood's creatures run and scuttle and wing our way through its dark heart.

Strength pulses in my bare feet as I run. Why did Zouza insist I wear boots, with their iron nails dragging my steps? With that first pain gone, I've never felt better, even though my teeth still ache. I press one hand to my jaw, but keep my tongue clear. I won't risk another cut. Why did she panic at every scratch and scrape and not let me touch blood? Never let me go to the village square on Blotgyre Day? I taste blood in my mouth, though I've drunk my water flask dry, filled it and drunk again. Still, I'm thirsty.

But here is the clearing I know so well and the cottage and beyond that stand of trees is the village. All is still, drowsy in the afternoon sun. I flit from the greenwood to the gate, to the door and inside. Bed, table, chairs and hearth; the familiar room seems smaller. It holds only one mystery, hidden beneath the low bed. I lift the poker, to help me reach it and the iron scalds my hand. I drop it with a clang and a curse. There's no fire to account for the heat, but blisters bloom on my fingers. How can it be?

I almost ask the cards, but I need only touch the pinwood and it will give me truth. Zouza's words whisper distraction in my thoughts: *cold iron holds the dead at bay, cold iron burns the wakened fae, cold iron, salt, and plaited may.*

I push my fear away and reach for the broom.

I crouch and sweep the birch besom from headboard to base. The box slides along the handle and clear of the bed. As it spins to a stop, the missing card appears beneath it. The Knave of Blood. I trust the card and understand its warning. It has come with the jaeger it represents. By the door a floorboard creaks. Truth in the wood. With a shriek, I fling myself away from the bed, broom flailing. The jaeger startles in his stalking and swings his sword too late. My frantic scrabbling roll fetches me up on the poker and I shriek again and jerk to my feet as it brands my knee.

Panting, I clutch the broom and eye the jaeger across the table.

"Stupid little squealing chit," he sneers, "so that's where she kept them."

He flicks his sword at the pinwood box, which flips and clatters on the floor. I watch his scowl spread as he realises the box is empty. His gaze comes back to me and the tip of his sword follows, waving in the space between us like a sharp-snouted snake searching for its prey.

"I want what's mine," he says.

"Yours?" I stare at him. "You think because you killed my grandmother –"

Don't call her that." He growls the words.

"You're nothing but a foundling she took in from pity."

"Pity? Did you know her at all? She saw –" But he doesn't care what Zouza saw in me, or in her cards.

"She wanted a girl, any girl, to replace Gretchen."

"You let her die." I echo her words at him and he flinches.

"I couldn't… She was hungry and she cried.

Father hit her to make her stop." His sword lowers as he whines his excuses, but he snaps it back up. "She shouldn't have cried. She was weak, like all little girls. Now, give me the dice."

"Zouza killed the man the blood die came from. I'll do the same to anyone who tries to take it from me."

"Idiot," he spits. "Do you think I don't know that? He was my father."

He jabs across the table, as I stare. I jerk back, not quickly enough. His sword draws a line of hot agony along my forearm and he grins through his teeth.

"The dice are mine. Give me them, now, or I'll spill all your blood and take them anyway."

I snort. He thinks me stupid enough to believe he'll let me live, to spread tales of his misdeeds.

"You couldn't find them. At the inn, when you killed her, you tore the room apart." I twitch my arm, distracted more by the scent of blood than the pain. "They're not yours. They don't call to you."

"You'd stolen them."

I shake my head. "They were under the cabinet."

"Liar." He snarls the word. "She killed my father. That's his bone."

I shrug. "Zouza killed a lot of people. They're mostly buried out back."

That startles him. I swing the broom, slamming it into his wrist. He curses as his sword clatters from his hand. He lunges after it, shoving a chair at me. It smashes into my knee and a shriek tears from my throat, but I grab the chair and fling it at his head. He brings up his sword in a great arc and kicks the pinwood box as he surges forward. The box slides under the table and the old chair explodes into kindling.

My arm feels on fire and blood coats my palm.

"How do you fit, jaeger?" I pant. "You say the bone was your father's and your father killed his child, Gretchen. But she was Zouza's daughter. Was Zouza your mother?"

He pulls his lips back from his teeth.

"Aye, so bleed your worthless blood. It's none of ours."

I am thirsty, so thirsty, but I say, "*Truth* – you are foresworn, that you hunt me for your own crime. Foresworn to kill your own mother. I'm no blood of yours or Zouza's. But I can smell the blood at the heart of the bone die. If it doesn't call to you, he was not your father."

"You're the foundling, the changeling," he cries. "Cuckoo! Whore's get! My mother went to Losset Ford to find a missing child. She came back with you." His eyes blaze, burning on a rich fuel of hatred, jealousy and greed.

"But that doesn't make me what you think."

I can't stop myself from raising my hand and licking the hot line of the wound he gifted me. His eyes widen and his lips pull back from his teeth in disgust. Before he can blink, I throw the broom at him, dive under the table for the pinwood box and come up in a crouch against the far wall.

Like a blossom opening in my mind, the pinwood shares its secrets.

Truth. I am a changeling.

Truth. Zouza bound my boots in iron to keep my faery nature sleeping, but made the red cap, as a badge of honour, for the Red Caps are the blood warriors of the fae.

Truth. She loved me, her substitute daughter, but she knew the day would come when I'd dip my cap in the blood of the dead and take to the woods. A day like today.

The jaeger shifts his grip on his sword and starts towards me, sneering.

"Don't you know what happened to the little girl in her red cap, who went to her grandmother's house, all by herself in the greenwoods?"

I rise from my crouch.

"Oh, jaeger, you have the story by its tail. You know Zouza wasn't my grandmother. Still, she knew enough to keep me a little girl, to stop me –" I grin and the sinews of my jaw stretch wide and wider. Preternatural. Aberrant. Bizarre. "– from growing into my cap."

"You're not –" He gasps and takes a step back.

"Not a little girl? Not human? No." My lips pull back from my teeth and my heart sings to see cold fear rise in his eyes, dousing the hatred. "You have the right tale, jaeger, but you make the mistake of thinking you are the wolf."

Gorgon Girls
Elise Kelly

Myths vary like fairytales, different in every mouth
Some say Medusa was hideous
Some say she was beautiful
I was taught that she was a monster, a mortal Gorgon, gorgeous and gruesome
The villain to a righteous hero

But she was always a woman first

Like Medusa, so many of us find stony defeat in our mirrored reflections
And like Medusa, when we are raped by a God who answers to no one, it is us who are made the monsters
The outcasts you won't look in the eye
The raging ruin who wails and rails
That more than just Athena's temple was desecrated that night

I still wonder which version of the myth is true
Did Athena change the ravaged maiden from fair-cheeked girl to snake-laden Gorgon
As punishment for being raped on her altar?
Or to protect her from more men who would dare to assault her
Did Athena shun and shame, or shield her with armour against those who would harm her
I wish it was the latter, but Athena was Zeus' daughter
And I know where Medusa's head ends at the ending of this story

Merciless Perseus who persecutes and executes Medusa
And yes, I know that Perseus did it for the sake of his mother
But must one woman be murdered so you can save another?
Perseus, your mother was raped by Zeus in her tower in a shower of gold that planted you inside her
Yet you kill the woman raped by your Uncle Poseidon
And take her monstrous lustrous head
Eyes still stony though she is dead on the field

Hang it to the front of great Athena's shield

There are women whose stories are mirrored and echoed
And even when they scream and shout, the fact becomes a myth which is written in doubt
A story that no court of justice will weigh against a God of Oceans

Gorgon girls, be Medusa as she made herself
After Poseidon, but before Perseus
Fill your gardens with the statues of your enemies
Make stone trophies of the men who tried to kill you, and take your body as a prize
Deal deadly devastation with a flash of your eyes
Wear a crown of snakes that makes men think twice before they fuck with you
After all, it was a serpent who told Eve that an apple a day keeps the cruel Gods away
So the next time a boy looks at you like Perseus Like you are a body waiting for his sword
Tell him Hey, my eyes are up here
Look at them if you dare

Juliet
Sue Clennell

I dreamt my lover was slain,
put to death by a machine that shot fire
from its mouth and was mounted on wheels
so it could move faster than you,
as things do in dreams
because your feet refuse to move.
It was like my wings were pinned to baize,
my nerves as transparent as jellyfish.
The monster was filled with self-loathing
and had an empty empty space behind its eyes.
I dreamt the monster was me.

Serendipity
Antonina Mikocka-Walus

Philyra was the only child of a poor miner and his consumptive wife. Other than their love, the greatest gift her parents offered Philyra was her unusual name. They hoped it would carry her safely through the meanders of life, towards a future brighter than their own. Alas, the name did not spare her tears after her pa was lost in a collapsed trench and her ma sank deeper into her illness. It made no difference when she scavenged for food among the rotten cabbages and mouldy carrots people tossed away on the cobbled streets. But Philyra had not been spoiled and would have faced this daily rummaging with resignation, if not for the fear her ma might lose the roof above her head.

Soon enough, the overman from the mine showed up for his rent. He was a bulky man, breathing heavily, though he came by carriage. His goggling bird-like eyes scanned the plain interior of the one-room cottage in hope of locating something valuable he could confiscate in lieu of the payment. He grunted, displeased, sighting a simple table, two hardwood stools, a tired bucket and an old bed. A slice of bread spread with a nearly transparent film of butter caught his attention. He grabbed it and packed his mouth full. Philyra's stomach rumbled. She opened her mouth to protest but the terror in her ma's eyes told her this was not the time to resist the inevitable. She swallowed hard. Yet again she would have to imagine eating a meal. At least in her daydreams she could dine like a princess.

'The cottage is the property of the mine,' the overman proclaimed, wheezing and slurping. 'If you want to keep it, one of you should report for work tomorrow at dawn.' He didn't spare them further attention.

Accordingly, in her eleventh spring, Philyra took up toil in the mine. Her bedridden ma could only sob into her hard pillow over her daughter's ill fate. The girl was of a slight stature, not strong enough to lift a pick, but her small size rendered her perfect for a scout. She was sent into the narrow corridors where adult miners failed to fit, in search of new digging sites. She worked hard but the overman palmed most of her pay, first to cover the debt accrued from the unpaid rent and later probably from force of habit. Only once did she dare to oppose him. She wore the marks of his rage for days. Later she overhead the miners talking. Scouts had a strange habit of vanishing into thin air as soon as they tried to assert their rights.

Each night Philyra's stomach turned as she recalled the pitch-black corridors, the foul air, the narrow walls which seemed to tighten around her as if they never meant to let go. But each morning she would scramble anew from the bed she shared with her ma, braving the new day. They needed the cottage, and she had by now realised there was nothing she would not do to keep her ma safe.

Like many child-labourers before her, Philyra would have eventually perished from overwork, a trench collapse or malnourishment, had not Lady Fate acted in her favour. Nobody knows why this fair lady gifts some of us with strokes of luck. Philyra's ma credited it to her daughter's name:

'When Lady Fate wanders through a town where all little girls are called Anna or Mary, she likes to stumble over a Philyra to kill boredom.'

But Philyra herself liked to think it wasn't undeserved. She liked to think it was a reward for something she'd done well.

Philyra's walk to the mine, a long, uphill and seemingly endless commute, led through the woods surrounding the cottage and then through the heart of the town. At the early hour, when the girl reached the marketplace, the clients were sparse and the stall owners busied themselves gossiping with each other. Philyra quickened her pace the moment the sweet aroma of warm raisin buns hit her nostrils. The citrusy freshness of orange zest, the smoky scent of roast ham, even the cauliflower tormented her for the remainder of her commute. The daydream the aromas produced was enticing; Ma and Philyra by their small table, the fire shooting joyously in the fireplace, large wooden bowls filled with lentil soup, a woman and a girl each savouring her dish without haste, the cumin, the thyme, the tarragon... She pushed away the visions which filled her mind. She couldn't afford any of these.

One day, as she dragged herself to work in the

murkiness of a damp morning and braced herself for a speedy pass through the market, the corner of her eye caught a pink stain. She glanced that way and spotted a new stall. The thin timber walls of the booth were painted a colour which reminded Philyra of the salmon her pa used to fish for. A tiny woman with dark ringlets, some haloing around her tan face and some bound high with an orange kerchief, was arranging fruits in symmetrical piles. Though all these colours appeared out of place in the greyness of late autumn, Philyra would have looked away and continued her commute, if it were not for the look and the smile the lady bestowed on her. Philyra froze as the stranger beckoned. She hesitated, but the stranger's eyes twinkled with so much merriment that she could not resist; joy was not something Philyra had in abundance.

  At first sight, the new stall resembled all other stalls which sold a bit of everything: some fruit and veg, some meat and bread, flours, barley and spices. Though, as Philyra eyed the products more closely, she noted they differed from those served at the neighbouring stalls. Where did the stall owner find ripe strawberries in autumn? Was there really such a thing as almond flour? And the apples, so fragrant, so…

  'Help yourself to my lovely fruits.' The stranger's voice was soft and as cheerful as her gaze. 'I am Samira.'

  'Philyra,' the girl introduced herself, not meeting Samira's eyes. She grabbed a small red delicious apple and took a bite. Her eyes shut of their own accord, her breathing slowed. The spring. The valley behind her cottage drowned in May flowers. A turquoise butterfly brushing against her palm.

  'How extraordinary,' Samira said, scrutinising her face.

  Philyra nodded her appreciation swallowing the apple's core, though she was not certain what Samira considered extraordinary. Did she mean the fruit or something about Philyra?

  The stranger's gaze shifted towards Philyra's broken fingernails and then to her dishevelled appearance. Her eyes turned misty.

  The girl reddened, stepped back and ran. All day in the mine her conscience troubled her. She should have thanked the stranger. On her way home, her back hunched from carrying the rocks which blocked the passage she was sent to explore, as soon as her feet stepped into the market place, her eyes leapt in search of the new stall. Samira was still there, though it was past twilight. And her mouth curved when she sighted Philyra. This was encouragement enough.

'I'm sorry I didn't thank you for the apple,' she whispered as soon as she reached the stall.

'My pleasure. You look like you've had a busy day.'

Philyra's eyes rested on the juicy slice of roast turkey. She swallowed, but made herself look away.

'Come closer.' Samira brushed the golden pears with her finger tips. 'Close your eyes and take a sniff. What do you see?'

Philyra drew a breath. Red leaves crushing under her feet. A spider web covered with diamond-like drops glittering in the sun. Children dancing around a fire, their faces ruby and plump.

'How lovely!' Samira clasped her hands and laughed. Her laugh sounded like the tiny bells attached to the sleighs the overman used in winter. 'Would you like to take some of the turkey and this loaf of bread home?

'I have no money to pay.' Philyra looked at the stranger with anxiety. Now was the time for Samira to push her away.

'That's all right. These are the leftovers I haven't sold. I'm ready to close the stall now. Come again soon.' She busied herself securing the stall for the night.

'Thank you.' Philyra's eyes filled with tears. As she reached her cottage, she noticed Samira had also placed two pears in her bundle. She asked her ma to smell the fruit before eating. Ma smiled for the first time since Pa's death. Philyra then realised that she had never spoken aloud of her daydream.

Her commute to work next day did not bother her as much as it usually did. The rain didn't feel half as wet and cold as yesterday. Passing through the market place she waved at Samira, now busy with some early risers, and the lady waved back. At night, as she walked back to town she promised herself she would not bother Samira today. It was too soon. Yet, as she reached the market, the lady beckoned, and Philyra hurried towards her, forgetting her resolution.

'I just want to smell,' she said as an excuse. She didn't want her new friend to think she was greedy.

'I have some plums today your nose might enjoy.' Samira chuckled.

Philyra reached for the fruit and was about to shut her eyes as Samira said:

'You may like to take a good look at it first. Admire the purple blush, the tender skin, the shape, so perfectly oval.'

'Like a quail's egg or a large walnut, but with a much smoother skin.' Philyra stroked the fruit with her fingers as if it was a duckling.

Samira nodded.

'What does it smell like?'

Philyra shut her eyes tight.

'A warm kitchen. An old lady stirring a pot. Hot jam, cinnamon, and nutmeg. A white kitten brushes his tail against the lady's leg.' She made sure this time she said it aloud.

'Well done! Even better than the last time but you need more practice. There is so little time.' Samira's eyes lost their focus, as if her spirit had travelled far away from the dark marketplace.

'Can I come again soon?' Philyra asked hurriedly. She still feared she might have dreamt the lady and her food stall.

'I'll see you tomorrow. I almost forgot, would you like some ham? There is plenty left today.'

*

It was on the eve of the winter solstice, when the thick layer of snow swaddled the little town like a fluffy quilt, when Samira asked Philyra to stay with her a little longer. Since Philyra had commenced her daily visits to the food stall, it always amazed her that while other merchants stamped their feet and rubbed their hands to warm up, the pink stall remained pleasantly warm no matter the weather. She often woke up earlier to help Samira to set the stall up for the day. She learnt about flours and grains. She knew how to choose the best apples and how fresh cinnamon should taste. Strolling through the marketplace no longer terrified her. She wasn't hungry anymore, and there were a few faces around which brightened on hearing her greetings. The winemaker and the cheese lady 'borrowed' Philyra from Samira every other morning for a quick consultation. A girl with such rare sense of smell was a godsend.

'You've been a great assistant to me the past weeks. And a great dreamer.' Samira smiled her charming smile.

Philyra grinned. Each product in Samira's stall had carved its distinct aromatic dream on her memory.

'I need to be on my way, my friend,' Samira said, and a shadow passed her face.

'When will you be back?' Old anxiety woke up in Philyra's heart.

'You must have guessed by now my life is a bit unusual. I'm given a task and after it's complete I need to move on. Lady Fate is a kind employer but she never gives me enough time. I always leave before I'm ready. That's how she likes it.'

Philyra paled. What would happen to her? How would she manage to survive the mine without her visits to the stall? The long corridors would become murkier and narrower.

'Don't even think that! You can dream a different future for yourself.'

She discerned affection in Samira's eyes. But the dream would not pay the rent, Philyra thought, trying to stop the tears rolling down her cheeks. Why would Lady Fate not give her another job?

'Lady Fate never gives sweaters when she can offer knitting needles.' Samira sighed. 'You have all you need to make a change. Come, drink a farewell chai with me.'

Philyra took a sip. The clove and cardamom settled her. No need to spill more tears. She was a different girl now. Samira had taught her how to trade, how to choose only freshest produce. She would speak with the winemaker and the cheese lady. They were good people. The cheese lady mentioned once she might be needing an assistant. And, the winemaker had told her his nose was failing him since his last bout of cold. She would resign from the mine and start working at the market. They would have to move out of the cottage but they would find another home. The winemaker was looking for lodgers, his house too large for him now since his daughter got married and moved out. Only, why did Samira encourage her to daydream? How would imagination help a stall assistant?

'It would help an artisan chef.' Samira's eyes sparkled as she read Philyra's mind like she did many times before. 'Hush now. Lady Fate would be displeased that I betrayed that much.'

As Samira embraced her for the final time, Philyra wondered what was Samira's actual task. Was it to introduce Philyra to other stall owners? To help her become a chef one day? Or was she here, because Philyra had an unusual name?

'Neither. I'm here to clear the path for the overman.'

'The overman? But he doesn't need Lady Fate's help!'

'He needed some help to be on his way to the place where he belongs.' Samira snorted.

'So, why did you help me?'

'Serendipity.' Samira grinned, and Philyra noticed this grin was less of a fairy's and more of a goblin's. 'And you are a good girl. You know what's right and what's wrong.'

*

As Philyra walked to town next day, the church bell tolled. With the pink stall gone, the market seemed ordinary again. Her throat tightened.

'How are you, dear?' the cheese lady greeted her with a smile on her wrinkled face. 'Ready for your first day of cheesemaking?'

Philyra nodded, smiling through tears. The church bell then tolled again.

'It's for the overman,' the cheese lady explained. 'He ate himself to death. And with what? With strawberries, of all things! Strawberries in winter. He got what he deserved.'

(sapphic) hymn to kali
Kerryn Coombs-Valeontis

so nimble with battle-fever
dark arms towers of truth's many hands
see you seizing the enemies of life
by the hair

arc of bountiful breasts swung with war
your cry curdling beaches running red
blades ambush (the air makes way)
on illusion

beautiful are the loins girded without fear
swift of vengeance for the innocent defiled
vanquishing mother of life taking back
her own

the truth against the world! your rally
defender cutting out tongues of half-truth
oud plucks dance-steps woven on the corpse
of the liar

Loving the Gorgon
Laura E. Goodin

"Eeee, here she is again, snakes and all," squealed the roast pig from its platter. "Oo, horrible, horrible!"

I tossed my head; the snakes became agitated. All the room's shiny things -- plates, goblets, weapons hanging unused -- writhed with the reflection of me.

The roast pig glanced toward the door. "Uh-oh."

I heard leather-sandalled feet on their way along the corridor. Jogging. Eager.

"This way," I called. The footsteps paused, then resumed at double the speed. The latest hero stumbled through the door, head turned to the side. His shield, of course, was highly polished. He raised his sword, trying hard to aim using the reflections.

"Wait!" I cried, weary of this tragedy, endlessly repeated. As the snakes moved in gentle inquiry about my head, I said, "Talk to me a while."

"What?" he said, with a panicky laugh.

"No? Then let me."

I began to speak. Marvels, dusty rooms, gravestones in dry-dirt yards, gilded onion domes in the sunset. I took him with me down stony corridors and over grassy plains, through jungles, over bitter-cold mountains, and to the suffocating depths of the sea. I told him jokes. I sang songs that made him weep aloud. In the end, I told him things I had never told anyone: anguish, fear, grief. I told him of my bright and righteous fury, the hot, brazen anger that brought jets of flame from the mouths of the snakes.

He had long since placed his sword on the ground. We sat, not quite looking, as I talked and talked. The reflection of his face in the shield, in the plates and weapons, in the copper samovar, glowed with yearning.

"Love me," I said, for the very first time. "Love my anger and my snakes, love my roar and hiss, for I am very beautiful in my rage."

"You are," he whispered. "I do."

I turned my head, just a little, and saw the tears, warm and wet, streaming from his soft, soft eyes.

"Don't look!" cried the roast pig.

But in that instant, the hero's eyes met mine.

As the snakes grew quiet and my limbs fell with the weight of sudden stone, and the tiny bones in my ears became ice-hard, the last thing I heard was the voice of the roast pig.

"Told you not to look."

Guinevere
Jena Woodhouse

By night you'd lie at Arthur's side,
the lion's peerless, pristine bride –
the wild Atlantic roiling at the bastions
with frothing lips. Your lord assured you
sorcerers and dragons did indeed exist.

By day you'd pace the walled courtyard,
listen for hooves striking rock, metallic
sounds of riders on the high causeway
to Camelot. You'd look for auguries
in spray, secret rainbows; charms in cups;
watch seals at play like sea-maidens
in the calm lee of the bluff.

Tintagel was akin to cloister –
bleak, austere, forbidding, lonely.
Women's voices trembled like thin
cries of sea-birds, and were lost.
No wonder you fell prey to passion's ardent
glances, courtly props – the rose, the nightingale,
the lute, the minstrels and the trysts, the plots…
Life was grey and melancholy
for a queen at Camelot.

No wonder you pretended not
to fall in love with Lancelot;
but then were doomed to wait
and watch and listen, loom a maze
of knots – untangling the thicket
of your wayward, captivating locks.

*Tintagel, on the north coast of Cornwall,
is the legendary home of King Mark
(of Tristan and Isolde fame), and is said
to be where King Arthur was conceived.*

Embroidered Map
Jane Frank

(attributed to Elizabeth Cook c. 1800. National Maritime Museum, Australia.)

I am measuring my own meridians
in linen, silk and kisses,
stitching along the Pacific routes
that sundered us for all those years.
My service to empire was our separation,
still is.

With no nautical almanac
I made my own calculations
as you stood with your sextant
night after velvet night
measuring the distance
of stars from the moon,
from the horizon,
from me.

They said you died on Valentine's Day.
When they arrived with the ditty box
the sailors carved,
with your lock of hair and the tiny painting
of your brave Hawaiian death,
I put aside the waistcoat
of tapa cloth I was making you,
cried into hard black skirts.

You found your longitude
but I've been measuring distances
ever since, and I'm tired of
suturing loss and years and stars.
I will burn our letters:
there have been enough discoveries.
I will finish sewing the world you found,
and sail to you.

Three Pieces of Gold, Three Pieces of Silver
Maria Haskins

The day Alma hears that the War has devoured her husband, she knows it's past time to leave the village. In all her lifetimes, she has never stayed this long in one place, and she hopes it's not too late to make it safely to the coast and find passage across the sea. Even as she listens to the man who delivers the message of her husband's death, she can feel the ground beneath her feet shift and tremble as the War closes in on her home.

That night, she gathers up her three daughters and tells them to pack a small bag each, no more than they can carry comfortably on their backs while walking. Her own bag is already packed, and she waits outside while her daughters flit around the house getting ready, all three of them anxious and red-eyed, pulling on their shawls and cloaks and walking-boots.

Alma has no money, but she brings three pieces of gold: a ring worn on the third finger of her left hand, and a hoop-earring through each earlobe. The silver she owns she is already wearing - two wide bracelets, engraved with runes, one around each wrist; and a plain, heart-shaped pendant on a chain around her neck.

For nigh on twenty years, Alma has never taken off her silver, wearing it as a reminder of the promise she made: to stay; to be a wife, a mother. Now, the metal feels strangely tight around her wrists, heavy around her neck, her skin itching at its touch.

The night deepens while Alma waits for her daughters. There is no moon, but her brown eyes are sharp even in the dark. She looks at the garden she's tended - weeding and watering, planting and harvesting. She looks at the clothesline where she's hung the laundry all these years, a forgotten towel whispering of dresses and baby rompers, socks and shirts. She looks at the winding road she's walked more times than she can count, headed to the village and the market.

These days, the village is almost empty. So many people have already left, fleeing the War, crossing the sea, heading for other lands, for strange and distant shores, that are safer than home.

Alma tucks the necklace inside her dress, pulls the sleeves down to cover the bracelets, but her skin won't stop itching.

*

When the girls are ready, they follow the pale gleam of Alma's shuttered lantern along the winding road. They walk away from the village, away from the war, toward the Drylands, toward the distant mountains, and the sea beyond.

The road is dusty and winding, trampled by many feet, and Alma smells fire and grief on the wind. The War is close. Too close.

At dawn, they rest beneath a creaky old oak at the edge of the Drylands. Alma looks down at the ground, at the strong roots digging deep into the dirt and grass and old leaves, holding on to this piece of earth. She looks up at the fading stars tangled in the branches and the indigo sky above. This is the place where she saw her husband for the first time, where she stood hidden in the dark and listened to his voice as he sang on his way home. She didn't love him yet, she just wanted to hear him sing, so she followed him.

He sang when he set out for the War, too. But having the voice of an angel did not save him.

Her daughters sit together below the tree, quiet but unafraid. She feels the sadness quivering inside them, a string plucked by their father's death, but they are not fearful even though they know something of the monsters that stalk the wilds. Even here, even now, they trust their own strength and hers.

Alma knows her daughters are not what most people would call "good girls", but they are good. Strong, determined, fierce.

So much like me. Too much like me.

The gold feels heavy and strange to wear, but she knows it won't last. Getting to the coast, getting across the sea, will cost her. It might even cost her the silver.

Alma searches out the locket between her breasts, feels that smooth heart resting against her skin, remembering the touch of her husband's warm and calloused hands when he slipped the silver chain around her neck. She allows herself one moment to hold on to that memory before she lets it go.

"We must keep going," she tells her daughters, and they nod and rise.

They know how far away the coast is - through the Drylands, across the mountains. They have seen the maps, but they have never been there. They have never run across jagged rocks and burning sand, have never had to take shelter in an old den to escape pursuit. Only she has the real map of scars and memories, to follow.

*

Alma's first gold earring pays for water in the Drylands. Her daughters are tired and thirsty, and the freshwater spring is guarded by men with weapons. The men are weak and few, but their weapons make them loud, make them think they're strong. There is a ragged crowd of people here, all of them fleeing the War, old people and children, men and women. Alma pays for all of them to drink, and while her daughters sleep, she looks at the moon's sharp sickle hanging low, scratching at the skin beneath the silver until her wrists bleed.

*

Alma's eldest daughter, Ayla, leaves in the foothills, when they've left the Drylands behind and the sharp teeth of the mountains bite into the sky up ahead.

"Don't stray," Alma says when they settle in around the campfire that night, but she can see how the darkness tugs at Ayla, how the wind whispers to her, how she longs for the feeling of sun and moonlight on her skin.

Alma knows that longing only too well, knows how small your life seems when there are so many places you could go.

In the morning the girl is gone, but an osprey circles high above, watching them, tilting its grey wings in the sky as it rises.

*

Alma's second gold earring pays for three mules to carry them through the mountains. The men selling the mules carry weapons in their belts, and Alma feels her voice sink and tremble into a growl when she talks to them. Restless, she claws at the itch beneath her sleeves, while the dogs the men keep to guard the camp, cower and whimper at her feet.

In the end, the men charge too much for the scrawny mules, but Alma is glad to leave, following the rocky trails into the mountains with her daughters.

They ride for days. The wind is cold, the rain pours down, they barely sleep. Alma stays awake every night, gazing up at the cloudy sky that offers no glimpse of either moon nor stars. Underneath the bracelets, her skin peels and burns and she cannot soothe it no matter what she tries.

*

Alma's second daughter, Malva, leaves when they have passed the mountain-summit and are heading down the steep switchback trails towards the coast.

It's early morning, and Malva sits by the creek that skips down the mountainside, its waters cold and clear as the sky itself. Malva dips her hand into the water, and Alma sees the flutter of fins and gills below the surface when she smiles.

"Don't go," Alma tells her, but she can hear the water calling to her daughter, knows that Malva already feels the flow and ripple and roar of the river it will become.

"I'll be back," Malva says, shaking her long hair loose from braids and ribbons as she walks away, smiling, following the creek.

When they ride beside the stream the next day, Alma sees the flutter of scales and eyes in the water between the rocks, and every now and then she glimpses a smile of sharp teeth beneath the rippling surface.

*

Alma's youngest daughter, Lillian, pulls her blue shawl tight around her head and shoulders in the wind and sits steady and sure in the saddle all the way down the mountain. They can see the ocean now, a glitter and haze along the horizon.

At the foot of the mountain, they sell their mules to a farmer, exchanging them for food and water, new boots for Lillian, and a night's sleep beneath a roof. The coast is so close now that they can smell the salt on the breeze, hear the call of the seagulls.

In the morning, Alma looks at Lillian, at the way she pulls her dark hair over her shoulder when she braids it, the way she rolls her sleeves up to keep them dry when drinking from the well, the way she squints at butterflies in the sunlight. She remembers holding Lillian to her breast after she was born, remembers how easily she slept through the nights, how she refused to smile at anyone new who came to visit. She is the same girl now as she ever was: quiet, steadfast, determined.

The gold ring is heavy on Alma's finger, yet it feels suddenly too light.

She can only hope it will be enough.

*

There is a small town by the sea, with cobblestone streets and many white-washed houses clinging to the cliffs, but there is only one boat anchored in the bay, and the captain and crew are hard at work readying the vessel for the journey.

The other boats have already left to make the crossing, the men gathered at the gangplank tell Alma. They scratch their heads and chins and look away when she glowers, but there are many people there, already waiting, counting their money, faces hollowed out by fear and hunger.

"One gold ring is not enough for two," the man demanding payment says. He's cleanshaven, with a smell of malice and decay about him that makes Alma's voice and teeth sharpen. She sees the glint of fangs between his lips, the glint of something else, something worse, something crooked and coarse in his eyes when he turns to Lillian. "And if you and the girl want life jackets, well, that's extra."

Behind them, the line of people stirs, muttering, restless. Alma's flesh trembles beneath the dress, beneath the silver. She is so tired of men, tired of the weapons they wield to make themselves feel strong, tired of pretending she is too weak to challenge them.

"You could wait another week," the man goes on, "but soon it will be too late in the year, the sea too dangerous for anyone to cross."

Alma thinks of her husband, devoured; thinks of Lillian, of the daughters she has already lost. Even here, by the sea, she feels the War approaching. Soon it will be here. Soon it will consume this town, these people. There is no way back. There is only the sea, and the crossing, and the hope of something better on the other side.

"Mamma, we can make it without life jackets," Lillian says, but Alma knows the sea, she knows it will claim whatever treasure it can take, just like any man or god or devil.

Alma gives the man her gold ring, slipping it easily off her finger. Then, she gives him her silver bracelets. They are harder to remove, clinging to her raw skin like a pair of long-worn shackles.

"Passage and lifejacket for one," she says, nodding at

Lillian. "I'll be back with more once I've talked to the money-lender in town."

The Beardless man curves his lips as if to say no, but he takes her gold and silver and passes it to the captain on the deck. Alma sees the Captain weigh the jewelry in his palm, studying the runes etched deep into the silver, tracing each sign with a blunt thumbnail. Her sharp eyes see through the Captain - the family he's lost, the drowned children he's gathered on the shore for burial, the small kindnesses he's given in his life. She isn't sure what he sees in her face when he looks at her, but in the end, he nods.

"It's enough. But we leave at daybreak, and we wait for no one."

The Beardless man shrugs, then grins at Lillian before he saunters off the dock, following a girl who could not pay for passage. When he walks past, Alma smells old blood on his breath beneath the aftershave, and a shiver runs through her from head to tail. She has fought enough monsters in her life to know what this man eats and what he hungers for.

"What's wrong, mamma?" Lillian asks, but Alma doesn't answer, she just strokes her daughter's braid, tugs at the shawl wrapped around her shoulders.

Should have brought her something warmer for the crossing, Alma thinks, considering the knits and woolens left behind.

"I have to go. Stay here. Hold your place in line and get on board as soon as you can."

"I'll hold a seat for you, Mamma."

Alma finds no words to say. All words seem too small and too big to contain what she is feeling. Instead, she takes off her silver necklace, pulling the pendant clear of her dress, slipping the chain over Lillian's head.

"Keep it safe."

"Mamma?"

There's a crack of worry in Lillian's voice, but Alma is already striding off the docks into the dusk.

*

Alma follows the road along the shore, toward the town, pursuing the scent of aftershave and blood. Free of the silver, her senses sharpen as everything else falls away, and looking back at the sea and the dock, Alma sees a tiny sliver of the future, lit as if by sudden lightning: Lillian, standing in the boat, steady and sure, getting ready to step off on the other side. Safe.

Safe, but for one thing.

Alma quickens her pace, her footsteps light as paws on the trail. The Beardless man is just ahead. His steps are heavy, his voice low as she speaks to someone. In the dusk Alma sees the girl he followed, a child no older than Lillian, and the man's hands are on her. The girl doesn't scream but Alma smells her terror, the jagged edge of it like a blade held at her own throat.

Beneath the moon, in the darkness, without the silver to hold her in place, Alma shivers. She thinks of the War, thinks of her husband, crushed beneath its bulk. She thinks of Lillian and the girl up ahead, thinks of the Beardless man looming over them.

The gold is spent, her silver's gone. She has only one thing left to give.

Alma bounds forward. The girl screams and runs away, but the man can't see Alma clearly yet, and when he does, it's too late for him to scream. She feels the last of her body shift and change, and in a flash of rage and grief and hope she sheds everything, clothes and scarf and shoes and skin, and this man is not fast enough, not strong enough, to resist her. No one ever has been.

*

After, Alma sits in the tall grass, watching as the boat

disappears into the shimmer between sea and sky, and she knows that Lillian is standing on deck, looking back. She feels Lillian move away from her, her scent dissipating in the breeze, in the smell of salt and fish and seaweed.

Maybe, Lillian calls out for her one last time, but Alma sits unmoving. There is no more silver to turn her now into the mother Lillian knew before.

There's a piercing cry, far above, and Alma sees an osprey, wings spread in the first light, following the boat. And in boat's wake, a ripple of scales and fins, following.

Alma feels the sun's first rays on her back, warm and bright like hope. She runs along the shore, a grey shadow in the grass, searching for another way around the sea.

*

In the boat, Lillian has long since stopped crying.

"Where's your mother?" the Captain asks, not unkindly, but Lillian only shakes her head, still grasping the silver locket around her neck.

A bird rests on the wind above her, following the boat, its beak and eye sharp as it gazes down. The waves get bigger and the boat is small, but Lillian isn't afraid. Beneath the waves, she sees a glint of fins and scales, maybe even a familiar smile.

Lillian smiles back and looks ahead with the weight of the silver around her neck, familiar and comforting like Mother's touch.

Magnolia
Eileen Chong

A son's birth means tragedy now.
'Song of the War-Carts', Du Fu

I rise from my pallet: it is still dark
and the men are asleep, their naked chests
inflating and collapsing like a smith's bellows.

The moon hangs beneath the clouds: soon
autumn will arrive, winds rippling the fields.
Back in my village, the farmers are preparing

for the harvest. I press together strips of linen,
line it with moss I'd picked from the base of trees.
It is my time, and my secret. Tomorrow we advance

towards the border. The war-carts are loaded,
the horses will be tethered to their burdens.
Here the quivers of arrows wait to be spent.

I carry a skin of water and squat in the grasses.
Now it is safe to loosen my robes.
Carefully, I clean myself.
Even in the dark, my hands are sticky with blood.

*

My first kill was a chicken. It was the new year.
Father handed me his knife and gestured at our hen.
She strutted around the yard, cocking her head this way

then that, scratching and searching for worms.
In the bamboo coop her brood of chicks cried warning.
I pushed up my sleeves and advanced. No fear –

we'd done this before, her and I. This was betrayal.
I carried her to the back of the hut, her heartbeat
pulsing in my palm. Her feathers so alive against my
skin.

*

My faithful horse bears me for many miles, carries me
into battle, comforts me with his touch.

Between my legs,
the saddle creaks my name: *Mu Lan, Mu Lan*.

Not for me the embroidered magnolias of marriage;
I give birth to nothing but blades, arrows and death.
My sword is my husband, my brothers my men.

They think me one of them. I drink sweet wine
fermented from plums; I curse and spit and plot.
I kill without mercy. Beneath my armour, secreted

in a pouch: a carved jade favour from the King.
In the night I draw my fingers across the dragon
twisting around the sun. The morning dawns emerald.

*

A soldier unfurls a banner and I plant it deep
in the soil. Another day, another frontier.
Men are busy at the fires: they grind millet

and cook it into gruel. So many mouths to feed,
so many sons, fathers, brothers… How much longer
before I gaze upon the lined face of my own father?

Beyond us, the mountains rise in mockery.
Wei is surrounded, corralled on all sides:
Qin, Zhao, Yan, Qi, Chu, Han…

If I were a hawk I would take off, wing towards
the west and the setting sun. I would hunt only
to survive, I would feather a nest, I would fly.

Notes:

The poem is based on a legendary character in Chinese history, Hua Mu Lan. This character was first recorded in *The Ballad of Mulan*, a work thought to have been transcribed around the 6th century A.D. in *Musical Records of Old and New*. While the original text has been lost, the tale has survived in an 11th century anthology, the *Music Bureau Collection*, which clearly attributes the source of the text.

Hua Mu Lan was a young woman who dressed as a man in order to take her father's place in battle. She rose to become a General during the Northern Wei dynasty (386–536 ad). It is said that she served in battle for a total of twelve years before returning to her village.

I have taken poetic license with the use of the seven Warring States, which were in existence during the Zhou dynasty (1046–256 bc) and not during the Northern Wei dynasty.

The surname of the character, Hua, means 'flower', while Mu Lan translates to 'wood orchid', or the magnolia.

Salt
Catherine Moffat

You won't find my name written down anywhere. My son's name is known – Moab, and my nephew, Ben-Ammi. Or are they my brothers? Sometimes I get confused. You'll remember my father's name well enough, but my name, Miriam – meaning 'sea of bitterness' and my sister's name Puah –'to cry or groan aloud' are not recorded. My mother too is nameless. She's known only as a woman who had regrets, a woman who looked back to see her past dissolving, a woman wildly punished for what seemed such a small misdemeanour – the woman turned to a pillar of salt – Lot's wife.

Lot. The last good man in Sodom and Gomorrah. A man so good that when the townsmen came to rape the strangers staying in his house, he offered up his daughters instead. 'They are both virgins,' he said. 'You can do what you like with them, but spare these men.'

Gee thanks, Dad. What a guy. No thought of offering up himself, though clearly it was men that they were after, and not girls. Perhaps that was the point. My mother tried to tell me it was.

'He has your best interests at heart,' she said. 'He wouldn't want to hurt you. He loves you. Don't talk nonsense against him. Do not be so quick to lay blame,' she said, every time I tried to talk to her about him.

My sister's been in therapy about it for years. Every so often she comes over to my place to berate me. 'You were older than me,' she says. 'You could have helped me. You should have done something about it.'

'What could I have done?' I reply. 'I was young, a victim too. Are you trying to block it out? Are you starting to believe those stories they told about me? You were there. You know what happened. Believe me, if I could have done anything to spare you what I went through, I would have. But I was helpless.

At first living in Zoar, it was not so bad. But then he became afraid. I guess after Sodom he'd had enough of neighbours and towns, so he took us up into the hill country to live in a cave. They were cold drear times for the three of us – living alone, never seeing another person from one month to the next, hating the days and fearing the nights.

'Come close to the fire, my daughters,' he would say. 'Cuddle in near to your father and never leave me. We have only the three of us left, the last of our people. We must remain together.' And then he would drink late into the night, cursing and muttering about damnation while my sister and I would lie there praying that this time, this time he would pass by on the other side.

When my body began to change, I didn't know what was happening. I was only just out of childhood, my mother newly dead. But by the time Moab arrived, born out of such pain upon the floor of the cave, I knew. And poor Puah, crying as I screamed and dug my nails so deep into her palms that they drew blood, understood too. And both of us knew that she would soon follow me to give birth in shit and blood and dirt upon the floor as she had followed me into so much other pain.

Even now, so many years later, there are nights when I wake shaking, remembering. And I think about rape – the only documented sin of Sodom and Gomorrah. What hurts the most is the silence and the lies. Puah's shrink says it's a classic case of victim blaming.

They said it was me. They said I made him drunk – too drunk to know his own daughter, too drunk to know when I lay down, and when I got up. And they said the next night I made my sister do the same. Who would believe such a story? They said we were worried about the family line dying out. But we were Jews, for God's sake. It wouldn't matter who we slept with. The heritage passes down the female line. We could have gone down into the valley, back down to Zoar and taken the first man we saw, if we had wanted sons.

Instead, they say we turned to our elderly father and made him so drunk he didn't know what was happening. Too drunk to know his own daughter, but not too drunk to get it up, apparently. With a little help from the wise virgins, of course. Did he think that angels had been sent to pleasure him? And from these two supposed one night stands both Puah and I conceived. You could call it a miracle.

But I'm a little sceptical of miracles these days.

Some nights I lie awake and wonder about my mother. I remember we were woken in the dawn. I remember the roaring and the smell of sulphur in the air, how my mother staggered as she ran, the way she urged us to 'run, run after your father. Don't look back.' I remember the look of terror on my father's face as Puah and I caught up and passed him, running ahead on our strong young legs.

I heard my mother call out his name.

He said she looked back. He said she was turned into a pillar of salt. But she was behind him. So how did he know unless he looked back himself? How did he know?

Sometimes I dream about my mother. I dream of her ossified somewhere out on the plains, those desert winds whittling her image away, grain by grain, blurring her features, and with her face forever turned away from me.

Prologue
Jaya Penelope

> I'm looking for the face I had
> Before the world was made ~
> William Butler Yeats

In the beginning there is darkness of course.
You know the kind of darkness
not the inside of a wardrobe in an unlit room

in a windowless house on a moonless night,
no. This is a shimmering dark, blue-black
edged with the beginning of stars.

Here, where the world is unmade
you are looking for a face,
a face you loved once, bright

too beautiful to remember. Your face
your raw furred face, fierce, bristled. It is dipped
in dark, flecked with blood this face you have before

the world is made. In the beginning
before flesh cleaves to bone, you're tired
you know how it is, like when your lover leaves

and even the air aches? All sounds
are intolerable, words/air/faces break open
cut you with their edges. You are split from earth

to sky. What a relief, to be formless
to slip through cracks in walls
to creep into things, like dirt, like God.

You have a way of seeping into things
the way the yolk of an egg is cradled
in its shell. In this beginning, there is

no myth for what you are living. You weave
your body, spin straw into gold.
There is only desire without object

and you spinning your body cell
by cell, measuring out the skein of your veins

the knitting of bone, the click of cartilage needles.

*You build your body from the ground up
scale and claw out of the earth. You scatter
moles like star clusters from your sieve*

*The hum of your body, the drum of your heart
the moon of your belly. What a delight
for a moment you are formless and then…*

AUTHORS

Aislinn Batstone is an Australian writer whose short stories have been highly commended in competitions and published in magazines and anthologies worldwide. She writes across genre boundaries with elements of romance, crime, speculative and contemporary fiction, but all her stories share her quirky humour and humanism. Aislinn spent her childhood in the Wide Bay-Burnett region of Queensland and later moved to Brisbane where she studied human sciences and philosophy at the University of Queensland. After completing her MPhil in Philosophy at St Andrews University in Scotland on a Commonwealth Scholarship, Aislinn turned to writing fiction. She has worked in various positions in tertiary education and project management while continuing to write, as well as raising a family with her husband. You can find Aislinn's stories on her website, www.aislinnbatstone.com, and connect with her on Twitter @AislinnBatstone. Now based in Sydney, Aislinn is working on a contemporary novel series set in Sydney's inner west in which a young couple come to grips with modern parenting.

Toni Brisland was born and educated in Wollongong and taught English and History at Figtree High, Kiama High and Merriwa Central before moving to Sydney to take up a teaching and counselling position at De La Salle Brothers Kingsgrove. After further study in management, accounting and law, Toni worked as a senior Human Resources Manager in the public sector and a Solicitor and HR Manager in the private sector. Toni commenced writing for children in 2010 and was a Director on the Board of the Children's Book Council of Australia. Her poetry has been published by Poetica Christie Press since 2012.

Emily Brewin is a Melbourne-based author and educator. Her first novel, *Hello, Goodbye*, was published by Allen & Unwin in 2017. Her second, *A New Day*, is due for release in February 2019. She has been awarded an Australian Society of Authors Emerging Writers' and Illustrators' Mentorship for her fiction writing and was recently awarded a 2018 Bundanon Trust artist residency to develop her third novel, The Piano. Her short stories have been short listed for a number of literary awards, including the 2017 Bristol Short Story Prize and Overland's Fair Australia Prize. Her work has been published in journals Feminartsy, Meanjin and Kill Your Darlings, and in Screen Education and Metro magazines.

Kerryn Coombs-Valeontis is an Art and Ecotherapist working in mental health. She runs workshops on Ecotherapy and women's therapeutic writing. She writes poetry as a response to life, with nature as a healing force and a return to the feminine, recurrent themes in her exploration. She lives in Sydney, Australia, but goes back to New Zealand, where she grew up, often. You could say she is a late bloomer, but then again, we can only bloom when we are ready. She has a B. Ed. and Masters in Social Ecology.

Sue Clennell has twice been a runner up in the Josephine Ulrick Poetry Prize competition, and her poetry has been published in newspapers and journals in Australia, New Zealand, the United States & Macau. She has been included in such anthologies as Appreciating Poetry, Best Australian Poems and Australian Love Poems. Three of her plays have been performed in Sydney & Canberra's Short & Sweet Festivals, and Cabramatta's MacArthur Festival. She has a Bachelor of Letters majoring in Journalism.

Eileen Chong is Sydney poet who was born in Singapore of Chinese descent. She is the author of eight books. Her latest full-length collection of poetry is *Rainforest*, from Pitt Street Poetry. Her work has been shortlisted for the Anne Elder Award, the Victorian Premier's Literary Award, and twice for the Prime Minister's Literary Awards. www.eileenchong.com.au Magnolia was first published in *Meanjin* (Autumn 2016), and subsequently republished in *Painting Red Orchids* (2016, Pitt Street Poetry, Sydney).

Therese Doherty lives in the Blue Mountains, north-west of Sydney, in the company of trees and birds. Sometimes stories and poems grow inside her, and she writes them down. She is particularly interested in writing and art that blurs the apparent boundary between the human and the more-than-human, and that evokes a sense of interconnection, interdependence, and wonder with the natural world. She also finds creative and intuitive writing to be a profoundly grounding and healing practice, enabling a greater immersion in the world, and a means of living more thoughtfully. If she could summarise what is most important to her in one word, it would be wildness. The Fisherman and the Cormorant is her first published piece. Therese blogs about creativity, nature, the vagaries of chronic illness, and all manner of beautiful and radical things at www.offeringsfromthewellspring.blogspot.com.au and can be contacted there.

Jane Frank is a poet and academic based in Brisbane where she lectures in cultural studies and creative writing at Griffith University. Jane's earlier background is in regional arts development, festival administration, project management and publishing. She is a previous Board Director of Regional Arts Australia. Jane's chapbook *Milky Way of Words* was published by Ginninderra Press in 2016, and a collaborative work – *Flotsam* – (with Scottish poet Hugh McMillan) is forthcoming with Flarestack, UK in 2018. Her unpublished manuscript *Dancing with Charcoal Feet* was highly recommended in the Arts Queensland Thomas Shapcott Poetry Prize in 2016. Jane's poems have been anthologised and published widely in journals including Antipodes, Australian Poetry Journal, Westerly, Writ, Cordite Poetry Review; f:oame, Pressure Gauge, Poetry Salzburg Review, The Frogmore Papers, London Grip, Takahe and elsewhere. Jane's poetry provides much needed oases in an otherwise frenetic existence of work and raising two energetic young boys. She relishes the freedom and possibilities of poetry, but also the discipline and the opportunity to distil experience. Her work aspires to find the surreal in the everyday and the historical – unusual juxtapositions – and also draws on her deep interest, and earlier qualifications, in art history. Palgrave Macmillan published the monograph adapted from her doctoral studies – *Regenerating Regional Culture: A Study of the International Book Town Movement* – in December 2017.

Embroidered Map was previously published in *Milky Way of Words* by Ginninderra Press in 2016.

Maddie Godfrey has been best described as "a poetry fireball". Their writing aims to facilitate compassionate conversations about social issues. At 22, Maddie has performed at The Sydney Opera House, The Royal Albert Hall, TEDx Women and Glastonbury Festival. In 2017 they were a writer-in-residence at St Paul's Cathedral in London. Off stage, Maddie's work has been published in literary journals, in magazines and on posters. Their poetry has also been used as an educational resource in classrooms around the world. Maddie's debut collection, *How To Be Held*, will be released in June 2018 by Burning Eye Books (UK). Maddie is not a morning person.
www.howtobeheld.com
www.maddiegodfrey.com
www.facebook.com/maddiegodfreypoet

The Goddess Texts All Her Exes was previously published in Underground, Issue 21; Mythological Figures, in 2018.

Laura E. Goodin, born in the United States, Godin has been writing professionally for nearly 40 years. She attended the 2007 Clarion South workshop and holds a Ph.D. in creative writing from the University of Western Australia; her academic research looks at the idea of genre tropes and the boundaries between genres in popular fiction. Her novels *After the Bloodwood Staff* and *Mud and Glass* are available from Odyssey Books. Her stories have appeared in numerous publications, including the Review of Australian Fiction, Andromeda Spaceways, Inflight Magazine, Adbusters, Wet Ink, The Lifted Brow, and Daily Science Fiction, among others, and in several anthologies. Her plays and libretti have been performed on three continents, and her poetry has been performed internationally, both as spoken word and as texts for new musical compositions. She has taught creative writing at Deakin University and in workshops internationally and online, and she serves as one of the editors-in-chief for Fafnir – The Nordic Journal of Science Fiction and Fantasy Research.

Loving the Gorgon was previously published by *Shades of Sentience* (web site) in 2009 and in their subsequent print anthology, *Shades of Sentience*, in 2010.

Maria Haskins is a Swedish-Canadian writer and translator. She writes speculative fiction and debuted as a writer in Sweden in the 1980s. Maria moved to Canada in the early 1990s, and currently lives just outside Vancouver with a husband, two kids, and a very large black dog. Her short fiction has appeared in Beneath Ceaseless Skies, Flash Fiction Online, Shimmer, Cast of Wonders, and elsewhere. Find out more on her website, mariahaskins.com, or follow her on Twitter, @mariahaskins.

Annika Herb is a writer and academic based in Newcastle, NSW. She holds a doctorate in English (Creative Writing) from the University of Newcastle, Australia, where she also works as a sessional academic. Her research and writing explores gender, female sexuality and identity, Young Adult Literature, and fairy tales. She was the Editor-in-Chief of postgraduate creative writing publication SWAMP Writing from 2014-2016.

Julie Kearney parents were larger than life people, both great yarners and hospitable in the extreme. They brought into her life a whole cast of exotic people who told stories in their turn. Story-telling was always going to be in her blood. One of her earliest forays into the world of language was as a researcher at Sydney University, tracking down Australian words for the very first Macquarie Dictionary. She writes fiction, memoir and literary reviews, and was shortlisted in the 2015 Queensland Literary Awards for her manuscript 3 for a Wedding, 4 for Death. Her work has appeared in various journals and anthologies including Cleaver Magazine (USA), Imprint, Griffith Review, New Asian Writing, and Shibboleth & Other Stories (Margaret River Press). She is currently working on a trilogy of historical novellas set on an island off the coast of Queensland. www.juliekearney.com.au

Elise Kelly is a Slam/Spoken Word poet, teacher, sci-fi and fantasy nerd, and history/mythology buff from Perth, Western Australia. An avid reader and writer since her childhood, Elise has always preferred to paint her pictures with words, (especially after her Primary school attempt at drawing an eagle resulted in what looked like a flying wombat). Elise is a regular performer at Spoken Word Perth open-mic nights, where she enjoys the company of supportive and like-minded wordsmiths. Her passion for progressive politics, social justice, and powerful language has seen her work published in anthologies and zines, including MoTHER [has words], 11/9: The Fall of American Democracy, and Underground Literary Magazine (Issue 21: Mythological Figures).

Gorgon Girls was previously published in *MoTHER [has words]*, issue 5 in 2017.

Tamara Lazaroff is a writer of fiction, creative non-fiction and poetry. Her work has appeared in journals in Australia, New Zealand and the UK, including Meanjin, Southerly, Feminartsy, Headland and The Wrong Quarterly, and has been audio-produced by Radio National. In the last few years she has undertaken residencies at Can Serrat International Arts Centre (Spain), House Conspiracy (Brisbane) and Arteles Arts Centre (Finland), and attended Naropa University's Summer Writing Program (USA). The Menkas is a part of her interlinked short story collection/manuscript In My Father's Village & Other Stories, which is set between the Former Yugoslav Republic of Macedonia and Australia, and deals with breaking free of memories, places, identities, and ways of thinking that limit or confine the spirit.

Kathryn Lyster is a MA Creative Writing student at The University of Sydney. Kathryn was born in South Africa and now lives in Sydney. Her first novel, *The Inevitability of Stars*, was published in 2013. She also writes short stories and poetry. She is currently writing a poem a day on her blog – www.kathrynlyster.com.

Antonina Mikocka-Walus is a Melbourne-based psychologist, health scientist, and writer. She was born in Poland and moved to Australia in her mid-twenties. She has been writing fairy tales, fantasy and science fiction for as long as she can remember. Her creative writing for children was published by Polish periodicals. In English, she has published nearly 100 research papers in international and national journals, but also numerous short stories for adults. Recently, her historical piece, *Secrets*, set during the Warsaw Uprising of 1944 has won The Birdcatcher Books Magazine Submissions Competition. Her popular science book, IBD and the Gut-Brain Connection, will be published later this year by Hammersmith Books. You can learn more about Antonina's writing on www.antoninamikocka.com. She can be contacted on Twitter @AntMikocka.

Catherine Moffat is a writer who lives on the NSW Central Coast. She's been published in literary magazines, on radio and in anthologies including The Mer-Creature and other stories, Things that are Found in Trees, Novascapes, The Lost Boy, Shibboleth, and the Hope Anthology. Catherine was the inaugural winner of the Hope Prize. She has won the Katharine Susannah Prichard Speculative Fiction competition, The Body in the Library prize, and the Wyong Short Story Competition. She's been shortlisted or commended for other prizes including the Margaret River Short Story competition, the Scarlett Stiletto, the Newcastle Short Story prize, and the Elizabeth Jolley Short Story competition. Catherine's story Salt is part of a series of Bible stories rewritten in the voice of female characters.

Joyce Parkes is published in Poetry Australia, Westerly, LinQ, Meanjin, The Best Australian Poems (UQP), foam:e, cordite, Plumwood Mountain Journal, Axon, Landscapes, Meniscus, Cuttlefish, and similarly dedicated literary magazines, journals and anthologies in Australia and in the UK, Finland, Canada, Germany, the US, New Zealand, Northern Ireland, Greece and the Netherlands. An opsimath, Joyce began to read feminist literature in her early forties. Her husband left. She kept reading, though paused to look at her bookshelves and noted that almost all books standing there were written by men. In her middle forties, she began to write and publish poetry. In the 1970s she was a member of the Western Australia Discrimination Commission – her portfolio, Employment, led her to discover numerous discriminations related to gender, race and age. In the early 1980s she was a committee member of the Fellowship of Australian Writers (WA). In the late 1980s she became a member of the Western Australian Cultural and Arts Policy (CAP) Committee, and in 1993 she was President of PEN Perth Centre. She is an Australian with a foreign accent and writes in her third language which is an advantage sometimes, sometimes not. Of course, she cherishes what men have written and wrought – of course an equal number of women need to be read, and heard, for we are as many.

Jaya Penelope is a poet, storyteller, spoken word artist based in Fremantle, Western Australia. She tells stories and performs poetry at festivals and other events throughout WA. She specialises in performing sacred women's poetry and stories, and in tales of feisty heroines for younger audiences. She teaches Creative Writing and poetry workshops in the community sector and runs Sacred Story and Women's Creative Writing Circles from her home. Whilst her first allegiance remains the spoken word, her poetry has been published in Australian journals and received airplay on ABC National's Poetica. She lives in Inanna's House, a women's Housing co-operative with her son and a small tiger striped cat.

Louise Pieper is a reader and a writer, a librarian and a lexophile. She's been told she's too smart for her own good, wears too much black, has too many books and reads too much, but she doesn't believe any of those things are possible. She does believe books can change the world, one reader at a time. She lives halfway up a hill in Canberra and half the time in imaginary worlds. She writes about fictional women - brave and strong, fantastical and historical, who are definitely not made of sugar and spice. Her short story, A Widow's Worth, will appear later this year in CSFG Publishing's A Hand of Knaves anthology. Find out more at www.louisepieper.com.

Dr Sarah Rice is an art-theorist, visual artist and writer. She runs poetry and art creative workshops and is commissioned to write poetry for art institutions and exhibition catalogues. Her full-length poetry collection *Fingertip of the Tongue* was recently published with UWAP. Her limited-edition art-book of poetry *Those Who Travel* (prints Patsy Payne) is held in the permanent collection of the National Gallery of Australia as well as other private and public collections. She won the inaugural 2014 Ron Pretty poetry award, the 2014 Bruce Dawe poetry prize, co-won the 2013 Writing Ventures, and 2011 Gwen Harwood poetry prizes, and shortlisted in the New Millennium Writings, Axel Clark, Yeats, ACU, Fish, Montreal, Tom Howard, Jean Cecily Drake-Brockman, CJ Dennis, Philip Bacon, Michael Thwaites and other poetry awards. Other publications include the Global Poetry Anthology, Award Winning Australian Writing, Best Australian Poetry, Long Glances: A Snapshot of new Australian Poetry, Island, Southerly, Contrappasso, Aesthetica, ABR, The New Guard, and Australian Poetry Journal. The poem Muse muses over who writes and who recounts history, for whom, and whose history is it anyway? What would it be to celebrate a history of the micro-moment, of the minute and the minute?

Muse was previously published in *Fingertip of the Tongue* by UWAP in 2017, and in ACT Write, volume 18, issue 3 in 2012.

Gail Willems moved from N.S.W. in 1969 for a holiday and ended up marrying a Western Australian and staying. She now lives in Port Bouvard, Wannanup a suburb of Mandurah. She is a retired nurse and has a daughter, son-in-law, three granddaughters and one great Granddaughter. She is a long-time member of O.O.T.A. Writers Group. Her first poetry collection *Blood Ties and Crack-Fed Dreams* was published by Ginninderra Press in 2013. Her works have been published in Australia, New Zealand Belgium, and United Kingdom, in journals, magazines anthologies, online journals, and Writers Radio.

Lilith was previously published *in four W twenty-seven New Writing*, 2016.

Jena Woodhouse is the author/ compiler/ translator of seven published books in various genres. She has received awards for poetry, adult fiction and children's fiction, and her poems were twice shortlisted for the Montreal International Poetry Prize. She has also been awarded creative residencies at Hawthornden Castle (Scotland); Camac Centre d'Art, Marnay-sur-Seine (France); The Australian Archaeological Institute at Athens (Greece); and the Tyrone Guthrie Centre (Ireland). Her forthcoming poetry collection is a chapbook, *Green Dance: Tamborine Mountain Poems*, published by Calanthe Press, 2018.

EDITORS

Sarah Nicholson is the creative director of The Heroines Festival. She is an academic and writer who teaches in literature, philosophy, creative arts, gender and religious studies. She is a past director of the National Young Writers' Festival, awardee of the Ian Potter Cultural Trust for Literature, recipient of a Writer's and Translator's Centre of Rhodes fellowship, and the 2017 Emerging Writer in Residence for the Katherine Susannah Pritchard Writers' Centre. She is the author of *The Evolutionary Journey of Woman* and an editor of *Integral Voices on Sex, Gender and Sexuality*. She is a board member of the South Coast Writers' Centre, and also the founder of The Neo Perennial Press, established as part of Wollongong Council's Creative Spaces program. www.theneoperennialpress.com

Caitlin White, a writer and artist based in Wollongong NSW, is the associate editor of the Heroines Anthology, Social Media Manager for Wollongong Writers Festival, as well as a freelance copywriter and blogger. She is the founder and editor of Baby Teeth Journal.

www.ingramcontent.com/pod-product-compliance
Lightning Source LLC
Chambersburg PA
CBHW050439010526
44118CB00013B/1593